ASK IT

ANDY STANLEY

ASK IT

The Question That Will Revolutionize How You Make Decisions

Revised and Updated from *The Best Question Ever*

MULTNOMAH
BOOKS

Ask It
Published by Multnomah Books
12265 Oracle Boulevard, Suite 200
Colorado Springs, Colorado 80921

All Scripture quotations, unless otherwise indicated, are taken from the Holy Bible, New
International Version®. NIV®. Copyright © 1973, 1978, 1984, 2011 by Biblica Inc.™
Used by permission of Zondervan. All rights reserved worldwide. www.zondervan.com.

Italics in Scripture quotations reflect the author's added emphasis.

Trade Paperback ISBN 978-1-60142-718-2
eBook ISBN 978-1-60142-719-9

Copyright © 2004 and 2014 by Andy Stanley

Cover design by Kelly L. Howard

Published in the United States by WaterBrook Multnomah, an imprint of the Crown
Publishing Group, a division of Penguin Random House LLC, New York.

Multnomah and its mountain colophon are registered trademarks of Penguin Random
House LLC.

Revised and updated from *The Best Question Ever.*

Library of Congress Cataloging-in-Publication Data
Stanley, Andy.
 [Best question ever]
 Ask it : the question that will revolutionize how you make decisions / Andy Stanley.
  pages cm
 Rev. ed. of: The best question ever. c2004.
  ISBN 978-1-60142-718-2—ISBN 978-1-60142-719-9 (electronic) 1. Christian life.
2. Decision making—Religious aspects—Christianity. 3. Wisdom—Religious aspects—
Christianity. I. Title.
 BV4501.3.S7314 2014
 248.4—dc23

                                        2014024059

Printed in the United States of America
2016

10 9 8 7 6 5 4

Special Sales
Most WaterBrook Multnomah books are available at special quantity discounts when
purchased in bulk by corporations, organizations, and special-interest groups. Custom
imprinting or excerpting can also be done to fit special needs. For information, please
e-mail SpecialMarkets@WaterBrookMultnomah.com or call 1-800-603-7051.

This book is dedicated to Lanny Donoho.
Solomon was right—there is a friend
who sticks closer than a brother. You have been
that kind of friend to me. Thank you.

Contents

Contents

Part 4: A Question of Morality

Part 5: Wisdom for the Asking

Part 6: The Best Decision Ever

Introduction

If Only...

I see that big question mark in your eyes.

Well, not really. I can't actually observe it from this far away—but I bet it's there. Most of us, most of the time, are weighing some big question or two or three concerning our lives, and we keep encountering new ones all the time:

Do I stay or go?

Is he (or she) the right one for me?

Should I buy this? Sell that? Start this? Stop that? Invest here? Commit there?

I know a question that makes it easy to determine the answer to all these others.

It's the question that answers just about everything for everybody, for the rest of our lives, and at every stage of our lives. It brings clarity and fresh insight for each decision we have to make. It pierces the fog of our self-deception and erases all those shades of gray that cloud our reasoning. It takes us beyond simple right and wrong, beyond what's merely legal, beyond the lowest common denominator.

And if we're honest with ourselves, God will use this question in the deepest parts of our lives to help take us to the place of our fullest potential.

Not only that, but it's a fairly easy question to answer. In most cases, you'll know the answer immediately.

Looking Back

This is a question that will save you a lot of time, a lot of money, a lot of stress, and—more importantly—lots of tears. I can even state the case this way:

Your greatest regret could have been avoided had you asked this particular question and then acted on your conclusion.

Regardless of whether it's an action or event you regret or an entire chapter of your life that you wish you could do over—had you evaluated your options through the lens of this powerful question, you would have avoided what may be your greatest ongoing source of pain.

As you move through the pages that follow, you may find that this single question could have changed the trajectory of your entire life.

It's a question I ask often every day. It's a question that guided me through my late twenties as a single man. It's a question that has served me well through twenty-six incredible years of marriage. It's a question I've taught my three kids to ask about every option that comes their way. They absorbed it, because it's the lens through which we learned to evaluate every decision we made as a family.

Over the past thirty years, I've had the opportunity to teach this principle to thousands of middle school and high school students. Many of them are adults now with children of their own. Letters, e-mails, and conversations assure me that this big question continues to serve as a decision-making filter for scores of these young adults.

When I share this valuable question with adult audiences, the response is nearly always the same: "I wish I'd heard this years ago." Translated: "I could have avoided some regret, if only..."

This single question serves as a lens through which you can evaluate all your options. It's a filter that casts things in their actual light. It's a grid that provides context for every choice. It will provide you with a new perspective on your love life, your career, your finances, your family, your schedule—everything. It's a question that will shed light on issues the Bible doesn't specifically address.

But it's not *always* an easy question to ask. Sometimes it can be a bit threatening, because it exposes so much about our hearts and our motives. But that's just one more reason it's so revolutionizing.

Looking Ahead

This book is divided into six parts.

In the first part, you'll be introduced to our big question. It takes me a couple of chapters to get to it, so be patient.

The second part explores some common (and dangerous) alternatives to asking our big question.

In the next two parts, we'll apply our question to two key areas of life: your time and your relationships.

Then, in the fifth part, I'll let you in on a secret known by all the world's best decision makers.

Finally, in the last part I'll challenge you to make a decision that allows you to get the maximum benefit from this question.

The principle behind this valuable question has impacted my decisions—and consequently my life—more than any other. This is more than another book for me. This is a life message. The content isn't simply pulled from a series of sermons; it's drawn from the years of my life's journey.

I hope you enjoy the book. More importantly, I hope this powerful question becomes a permanent part of your decision-making process. If you have the courage to ask it, your heavenly Father will use this simple question to guide and protect you in the days to come. And as you experience the significant difference this question makes, I think you'll agree that it's one you'll want to keep asking for the rest of your life.

Part 1

The Question

Dumb and Dumber

Finding Common Ground

You and I have something in common. We've both done some really dumb stuff. Stuff we hope nobody ever finds out about. Stuff we wish we could forget. There's money we wish we hadn't spent, cars we wish we had never bought, investments we wish we hadn't made, invitations we wish we hadn't accepted, relationships we wish we had stayed out of, jobs we wish we had never taken, partnerships we never should have entered into, phone calls we never should have returned, contracts we never should have signed.

If you are like me, you look back and wonder, *How could I have been so dumb? So blind? So foolish?* We should have known better. In some cases, we did know better, but for some reason we thought we could beat the odds—that we would be the exceptions to the rule. In spite of what common sense (and maybe a friend or two) told us, we believed we could control the outcomes of our decisions. So we followed our hearts, we trusted our emotions, we did our own thing, and now we wonder what in the world we were thinking.

If you're like most people, some of the decisions you wish you could unmake led to chapters of your life you wish you could go back and *unlive*. Picking a stock based on a bad tip is one thing; choosing a marriage partner without doing some due diligence is something else entirely. Making four $24.95 payments on something that's only worth $24.95 to begin with is embarrassing; $25,000 in credit-card debt can ruin you.

Some of our bad decisions simply embarrass us. Others scar us.

What's obvious now wasn't so obvious then. And what's obvious to us now may not be so obvious to everybody around us. Chances are, you've already bumped into somebody on the verge of making the same dumb decision you made when you were his age. And, as I was, you were sure that once he heard your sad story, he would drop to his knees in gratitude for your life-changing insight. Having come to grips with the error of his ways, he would immediately reverse course, call off the marriage, pay cash, tear up the contract, dissolve the partnership, sell his drums, stay in school, or whatever.

But no. Instead, he endures our tales of woe, thanks us for the unsolicited advice, and continues full speed ahead into the oncoming train. And we think back and wonder, *Could I have possibly been that naive? That stubborn? That foolish?*

Yep.

Poor Planning

When we watch people we know—or strangers for that matter—make foolish decisions, it's as if they are strategically and intentionally setting out to mess up their lives.

After all, it takes a lot of planning to marry the wrong person. Any marriage, even a bad one, is not a casual endeavor. Think of the time and energy it takes to set up a doomed business partnership or to start a business that has no hope of success. Think about all the paperwork people have to wade through to purchase houses they can't really afford or lease cars they are going to lose or apply for loans they can't repay.

Having watched dozens of people methodically waste their lives, potential, and money, I've concluded that while nobody *plans* to mess up his life, the problem is that few of us *plan not to.* That is, we don't put the necessary safeguards in place to ensure happy endings.

Nobody plans to destroy her marriage, but few people take precautions that guarantee "as long as we both shall live."

Nobody plans to raise irresponsible, codependent children,

but it's clear from looking at society that a bunch of parents didn't plan not to.

Nobody plans an addiction, but it happens. Why? A lack of necessary precautions.

I haven't talked to anyone who planned to be buried under a mountain of credit-card debt, but I've met a lot of people who didn't plan not to be.

Our poor planning leads precisely where we had no intention of going. And once there we ask, "How did this happen to me?"

The answer to that comes by asking another question that's far better—the question this book is all about.

Better yet, this question will help you stay out of the situations and circumstances that rob you of your potential, your opportunities, and your future.

A Most Uncomfortable Question

And the Courage to Ask It

At the age of twenty-five, I came across three verses in Scripture that totally changed the way I made decisions. I suddenly had a new filter through which to evaluate every opportunity, invitation, and relationship—everything I was asked to do, everything I was tempted to become a part of. I began to consider my whole life through this new grid, a grid that boiled down to asking one simple question.

The reason I consider it such a uniquely valuable question is that it has the potential to *foolproof* every aspect of your life. It will give you a new perspective on your love life, your career, your finances, your family, your schedule—everything. This question sheds light on issues the Bible doesn't specifically address. It provides you with a context for addressing questions of where to draw the line morally, relationally, and ethically. Like a piercing light, this powerful question cuts through the fog surrounding so many of your decisions and enables you to see clearly.

And yet, as you are about to discover, it's not an easy question to ask. It's not that the words are difficult to say. It's just that the question exposes so much about your heart and your motives that it is, well, just not an easy question to ask. It's like walking out of a dark building on a sunny day—there is something about this question that will make you want to retreat to the shadows where your eyes have already adjusted. Like direct sunlight to the unshielded eye, this question can be extremely uncomfortable.

Here's why.

The Art of Self-Deception

You see, in addition to making the occasional dumb decision, you and I have something else in common: We are good at deceiving ourselves. Really good.

Self-deception comes naturally to me. I can make a bad decision look and sound like a great decision with one hand tied behind my back. I can make a poor financial choice sound like an investment opportunity. I've made poor relationship decisions sound like ministry opportunities. I've missed countless workouts under the guise of "I need my rest." I've rationalized gallons of ice cream with the phrase "Everybody needs to live a little," as if ice cream adds to the quality of life. I've wasted massive amounts of time doing all kinds of things that seemed important at the time but had no cumulative value. And given enough time, I can even find a Bible verse or two to support my foolishness.

Every kind of addiction begins with similar self-deception:

"This won't hurt anybody."

"I'll only do it once."

"I haven't had any for a week."

"I'll be careful."

"I can handle it."

"I can quit whenever I want to."

Sound familiar? Chances are, you don't have to think past last week to come up with a bad decision or two that you talked yourself into. Probably some of your greatest regrets started with choices that you convinced yourself were good ones. But, in fact, you were actually robbing yourself. Your bad choices ended up costing you relationally, financially, and maybe even spiritually.

And the strange thing is, most of the time we are fully aware of the game we're playing. The fact that we have to give ourselves a reason or excuse at all ought to tip us off. Think about it. You don't have to go through a series of mental gymnastics to convince yourself that it's a good idea to eat a serving or two of vegetables every day. You never have to rationalize why you ought to exercise, save money, or avoid bad company. You just know. You don't sit around looking for reasons to do the right thing; it's the bad decisions that require creative reasoning.

Reading the Gauges

This human habit of self-deception can make our big question so uncomfortable to ask. This question exposes the irrationality of our excuses. It reveals our true intent. It penetrates the walls of rationalization behind which we are prone to hide. It dismantles the arguments we use to keep the truth at arm's length.

All of which is fine if you really want to do what is right. But this little question can become a nuisance on those occasions when, instead of trying to make a right decision, you are trying to make a decision right. On those occasions, this question has the potential to aggravate as well as illuminate. Because of that, it is very important for you to pay close attention to your emotional response. Your reaction to this dynamic little question will tell you a great deal about yourself. And this is one lesson you cannot afford to miss.

The Slippery Slope

Why Everybody Goes There

L et me take you now to those verses that altered forever the way I make decisions. We find them in the apostle Paul's first-century letter to Christians residing in the city of Ephesus. You know it as the book of Ephesians.

The letter opens with an inspiring reminder of the believer's new identity that resulted from being adopted into the family of God. For three chapters the author expounds on all the benefits of being "in Christ." Beginning in chapter 4, however, Paul turns a corner.

He begins the second half of the book with this plea: "I urge you to live a life worthy of the calling you have received" (Ephesians 4:1). In other words, live your life in a way that reflects the changes God has made in you. Or as a friend of mine is fond of saying, "Don't live the way you used to live. After all, you are not the person you used to be."

From there, Paul launches into one of the most practical sections in the Bible. He talks about everything from sex to marriage to alcohol to...you name it. He gives instructions on what is permissible to talk about, think about, and even laugh about. The entire discussion is intense, thorough, and, frankly, somewhat overwhelming.

Gimme Traction

Paul goes so far as to suggest that we become imitators of God! My gut response? *Yeah, right. Not in this lifetime.*

It's not that Paul's list of lofty standards isn't worth striving toward. It's just that I know me. I'm not that good, that consistent, that disciplined. Besides, just about everything in Paul's list runs directly against the cultural current. So let's face it; I'm not going to get any support out in the real world.

Read Ephesians 4 and 5 for yourself. It's an incredible catalog of virtues and values, the stuff parents preach to their children all the time. But is it realistic? Can anybody really pull it off? At first glance, I think not.

The good news is that Paul anticipated the frustration of his readers. So he incorporated into this intimidating list of what-to-do an invaluable *how-to-do-it*. Specifically, he unveiled an approach to life that, if embraced, will set us up for success as we attempt to live out the values he listed. And it's from this short but powerful piece of instruction that we derive the question this book is all about.

Here's what Paul wrote:

> Be very careful, then, how you live—not as unwise but as wise, making the most of every opportunity, because the days are evil. Therefore do not be foolish, but understand what the Lord's will is. (Ephesians 5:15–17)

Life changing, huh?

No? Okay, let's break it down.

Here in the opening phrase, with that little word "then" (or "therefore" in some versions), Paul is linking what he's about to say with what he just said before—where he described what we *need* to do. Now he connects that with an explanation of *how* to do it. It's as if he's saying, "If the values and practices I've outlined, as overwhelming as they may seem, are things you desire to embrace, if something in you stirred when you imagined living out those standards, if you want to live life on an entirely different plane, then here's what you need to do."

Then Paul reveals the principle that gives all of us wannabe

Christ followers the traction we need to live out what, at times, seems out of reach:

"Be careful, then, how you live."

Or to turn it around, *Don't be careless how you live.* In other words, following Christ is not a casual endeavor. It requires extreme caution. If we are serious about living out the values the New Testament teaches, we must watch our steps. After all, we know from experience how easy it is to stumble.

Then without so much as a pause, Paul discloses the criterion by which we are to measure and judge every one of our choices. In the six words that follow, we are given the grid through which we are to evaluate every invitation and opportunity. Here is the standard, the yardstick by which we are to assess our financial, relational, and professional decisions. Get out your highlighter.

"Not as unwise but as wise."

The question that sets us up for success where it counts, the question that enables us to consistently apply the commands of the New Testament is this:

What is the wise thing to do?

Wait a minute. How could *that* possibly be such a critically important question? How could that be the key to consistency in our walk with Christ? To understand the potency of this question, we need to examine the way we're used to evaluating our options.

We're Asking the Wrong Questions

Typically when making choices, we run our options and opportunities through a more generic and far less helpful grid. There are several variations, but the question we ask ourselves is this: *Is there anything wrong with it?*

The assumption is that if there is nothing *wrong* with what we're doing, it must be okay. If it is not illegal, unethical, or immoral, then it qualifies as a live option, right? Biblically speaking, if there is not a "Thou shalt not" associated with it, then it's safe to assume it qualifies as a "Thou certainly shalt if thou please."

Unfortunately, that kind of thinking sets us up for another question that we rarely verbalize or even allow to surface to the level of conscious thought. Yet, if we are honest, this question drives far too many of our choices. It goes something like this: *How close can I get to the line between right and wrong without actually doing something wrong?* The Christian version goes like this: *How close can I get to sin without actually sinning?*

Every teenage guy has asked this question in some way at some point in his dating career. Everyone on a diet asks this question every day. Attorneys make a living asking this question on behalf of their clients.

But it doesn't stop there. Inevitably, once we have come this far, we find ourselves asking, *How far over the line between right and wrong can I go without experiencing consequences?* In other words, how unethical, immoral, or insensitive can I be without suffering any unmanageable outcomes? How long can I neglect my family, finances, or professional responsibilities without feeling the effects? How far over the speed limit can I drive without getting pulled over? How far can I indulge in an addictive behavior without actually becoming addicted?

It is a slippery slope, both subtle and sinister. It all begins so innocently by asking what seems to be a noble question: *Is there anything wrong with it?* But it ultimately leads to yet another question. One we have all asked at one time or another: *How did I get myself into this mess?*

Damage Control

It's a question I have heard dozens of times. Heck, I've asked myself the same question a dozen times or more. How in the world could someone as smart and biblically astute as I am get myself into—well, it's really none of your business what I've gotten myself into. Let's talk about you, or Fred.

Fred is one of smartest guys I've ever met. Unfortunately, by the time I met him, he was attempting to navigate through a labyrinth of sexual addictions, bankruptcy, divorce, and a child custody battle. For forty-five minutes, he poured out his heart. He told me how he and his wife met: he saw the warning signs but ignored them. He told me about his business partner: again, he saw red flags but moved ahead anyway. He described his early experiences with pornography: he knew the dangers, but figured he would be the exception.

Every bad choice Fred made could have been avoided if only he'd asked our big question. His was not an IQ problem. As is the case with most people, his nightmare began with the assumption that he could dance on the edge of moral, relational, and professional disaster and beat the odds. If it wasn't technically "wrong," then it must be "right." Right?

Fred launched into the process of rebuilding his life and marriage. He learned to ask a different set of questions. Things got better, but his new perspective couldn't quickly erase the pain he'd caused his wife and daughter. Restoring lost trust takes a long time.

As a pastor, I've heard more than my fair share of heartbreaking stories. Yet every bad decision I've ever heard about could have been avoided if someone had simply asked the valuable question we've identified. Every single one. Adultery, addictions, unwanted pregnancies, bankruptcies, you name it. All could have been avoided with a proper application of this question.

The moral of the story is, just because there isn't a "Thou shalt not" attached to a situation does not necessarily mean it is a "Thou shalt." What's morally and culturally permissible is often not what's best for us.

Like a good father, God wants what's best for each of us. So he has given us a standard that goes beyond the cultural norms. He has given us a question that enables us to live out the values that lead to what Jesus referred to as an abundant life (see John 10:10). Not a barely-get-by life. Not a life of regret. *An abundant life.*

But the question he gave us is not, *Is there anything wrong with it?* The question is, *Is it the wise thing to do?* To foolproof your life, you must ask it of every invitation, every opportunity, every relationship.

What is the wise thing for me to do?

Think back for a moment to your biggest regret. That event or chapter of your life you wish you could go back and undo or relive. What was the decision you wish you could reverse? The relationship you wish you could do over? Can you see how some or all of what you regret could have been avoided if you had asked and applied our question?

From this moment on, you can avoid the mistakes of the past and live regret-free by making it the habit of your life to ask this question.

Climate Control

It's a Myth

Our heavenly Father never intended for us to live life at the level of what's permissible, legal, acceptable, and not prosecutable. To do so is tantamount to organizing our lives around the question, *How close can I get to sin without sinning?* Now *there's* a standard.

Instead, we are meant to analyze every opportunity and invitation through the lens of wisdom. Every choice should be tested by asking, *What is the wise thing to do?* This is what Paul was getting at when he admonished us to be careful how we live.

Speaking of Paul, in the last chapter we cut him off in midsentence, so let's pick up where we left off. After telling his audience to walk wisely, Paul went on to say:

"Making the most of every opportunity, because the days are evil."

Evil days? I guess some things never change. If you visit the ruins of Ephesus, you can still see phallic symbols etched in the stone walkways, marking the path to the pagan temple. The temple was supported through prostitution. In fact, sex was an integral part of the pagan worship rituals. Drunkenness was encouraged as well. So, as you might imagine, the men of Ephesus were religious zealots. *Nobody* missed worship. And it wasn't the music or the preaching that drew the crowds.

Apparently, some of the Christians in Ephesus were being drawn back into their former ways. Why settle for a sermon when you can…never mind. Anyway, they were attempting to blend the old with the new. They were blurring the lines. And some were beginning to suffer the consequences of their actions. So Paul went right to the heart of the matter.

"You can't be careless!" he warned. "You don't live in a morally neutral environment. If you aren't on your guard, the culture will sweep you right back into the chaos from which you have been rescued."

Asleep at the Wheel

We don't live in a morally neutral climate either. Every day we interface with a culture of sensuality, gluttony, and greed. Ours is a culture that encourages us in the most provocative ways to do everything in our power to try to satisfy appetites that can never be fully and finally satisfied.

These are evil days. Gone are the days when you had to go looking for trouble. Trouble is on every street corner, on every page of just about every magazine. Trouble is dripping from every billboard. Trouble drives across our television screens and calls to us from our computers.

Zero percent financing!

The titles of the movies you select will not be listed on your bill.

Buy one; get one free!

Mortgage rates are lower than ever!

Try it for 30 days risk-free!

Girls gone wild!

Most Americans are overweight and overleveraged. We eat too much and spend too much. By far, the biggest online money-maker is pornography. Consider this: American men spend billions of dollars every year to look at pictures of women on their computer screens. *Billions of dollars.*

Again, we do not live in a morally neutral environment. The world we live in is much like the grassy area outside my kitchen door where I let my dog out to do her business every night. If you're not careful how you walk, you'll step in it.

That's a little gross, but you get the point. Like the Ephesians in Paul's day, we live in morally and ethically perilous times. The days are evil. If you don't pay attention, you will end up paying a price for your carelessness. If you aren't intentionally cautious, you may end up unintentionally corralled by some vice you've always condemned. If you don't filter your choices through the powerful question we're exploring here, you will find yourself face-to-face with consequences that could have been, and should have been, avoided.

This Is Your Wake-Up Call

I know the question is annoying. After all, it forces you to face up to what you have spent years of time and energy trying to ignore. It's like an alarm clock for your heart, a wake-up call for your soul. It's irritating, but necessary. Perhaps it was the universal propensity to wear out our snooze buttons that drove the apostle Paul to continue with these words:

"Therefore do not be foolish."

If punctuation had been available in the first century, I imagine that this phrase may have come with double exclamation points. "Do not be foolish" is a polite way of saying, "Don't be a fool! Don't approach life as if you lived in a morally and ethically neutral environment!"

Then Paul commands us to do something that on the surface appears to be impossible.

"But understand what the Lord's will is."

You can't command someone to understand something, can you? I had a Greek teacher in college who would have us come up to the front of the room and translate out loud for the class. There

I was with my paperback copy of *The Iliad,* standing in front of my peers and bluffing my way through some incident in the Trojan War, filling in the gaps with my own editorial comments. When it became evident that I was no longer translating but merely telling the story from memory, the teacher would stop me and say, "Mr. Andy, I don't think you are reading." Busted.

"You are right, Mrs. Cuntz," I would reply. "I can't translate it."

Her reply was always the same. "Yes, you can! Now translate it for us."

"I really can't."

"Yes, you can. Now translate."

She would always insist that we understood more than we did, as if her insistence would somehow increase our capacity for the Greek language. It never did. Eventually she would allow us to give up and return to our seats. I always felt like Mrs. Cuntz took my ignorance personally. Funny, it never seemed to bother me. Oh well.

Whenever I read Paul's admonition to "understand what the Lord's will is," I always think of Mrs. Cuntz exhorting us to *understand* Homer. Both seem like a waste of time. You can rah-rah an athlete to perform better, but you can't rah-rah people into knowing something they don't know.

So what was Paul's point? Why didn't he say, "*Discover* what the will of the Lord is"? Or perhaps "*Obey* the will of the Lord"? We could move on either of those. But why *understand*?

Face-Off

Paul's command to "understand" God's will is really an exhortation to *face up to* what we know in our hearts God would have us do. As I mentioned earlier, people are masters in the art of self-deception. So Paul, leveraging the grammar of his day, reaches off the page, grabs us by the collar, yanks us up close, and shouts, "Quit playing games! Quit pretending. Quit rationalizing. Ask the question, and embrace the answer!" This is Paul's final attempt to get us to admit what we know in our hearts to be true—to admit that we generally already know what God would have us do.

One reason we don't admit certain things to ourselves is that it helps us avoid the guilt that naturally follows from not doing what we know we should. This is why most Americans eat so unhealthily. It's not *just* a lack of discipline. Americans haven't really faced up to the reality of what the foods they eat are doing to their bodies. How do I know? Because I've seen how quickly the diet changes once someone has had a brush with cancer or heart disease. Lumps, clogs, and shortness of breath force a person to face up to what he or she has refused to acknowledge for years. And the revelation leads to death-defying discipline.

But lifestyle changes don't happen until an individual faces the facts. It is not until a person acknowledges the truth and quits lying to himself that something positive takes place. And once someone has turned the corner mentally, it's amazing how quickly that person is able to break unhealthy habits and begin new routines.

Every person I know who has undergone this kind of transformation after a health scare says the same thing: "I should have made these changes years ago."

Translated: "For years I refused to face up to what I knew in my heart was true."

Bankruptcy can have the same effect. So can an unwanted pregnancy, a letter from your spouse's attorney, a DUI charge, or a trip to detox with one of your kids. And perhaps that's what it will take. There is something out there somewhere that will get your attention. Unfortunately, that something may scar you as well as scare you. You may be left with limited options and reduced opportunities. So why let things go that far? Why not face up now to what you know in your heart your heavenly Father wants you to do?

Why not start taking seriously our question—and *ask* it?

Stemming the Tide

Avoiding the Undertow

When I was a kid, we lived in Miami. Every summer we would pull our eighteen-foot travel trailer to Naples, Florida, for a week of vacation. If you've been to Naples lately, you know the waterfront is lined with condos and hotels. But in 1968, there was nothing but miles of empty beach. So my dad would actually pull out onto the beach and drive along the tree line where the sand was firm. Then we would drive for miles until we found a suitable place to set up camp.

Although I was in elementary school at the time, I still have a vivid memory of something that happened during one of our weeks on the beach. That particular year the undertow was ferocious. It wasn't dangerous, in the sense that the undertow might pull you out to sea, but it would carry you down the beach in no time. I still remember playing in the water, looking back toward the shore, and our trailer not being there! Why would my parents move the campsite? Of course they hadn't moved—I was forty yards down the beach from where I had stepped into the water. It was the undertow.

Well, after a couple of days of looking out from the trailer and wondering where his kids had drifted off to, my dad came up with a novel idea. He gathered about twenty coconuts and made a neat little cannonball-like stack about thirty yards down the beach from where our trailer was parked. The coconuts were to serve as a reference point. Once we drifted past the coconuts, we were to get out of the water and walk back to the point where we were even with the trailer, and then we could swim again. And it worked.

You may already know where I'm going with this. Like the undertow at Naples, culture has a way of subtly sweeping us beyond healthy moral, ethical, and financial limits. That accounts for the times when we have looked up and said, "Who moved the trailer?" Or rather, "How did I get myself into this situation?" When everything around you is drifting along at the same rate, it's easy to be fooled into thinking that you're standing still. Without a stationary reference point, it is impossible to ascertain where you are, where you aren't, and where you ought to be.

So let's stake out some stationary reference points.

Specifically, we're going to ask our question in three different ways. Each version will provide you with a unique perspective on the choices you are currently making. Approaching the question from three different angles will provide you with a point of reference that will give you valuable, if not bothersome, insight into where you are and where you are headed.

Ready? Here we go.

Looking Back

Poet and philosopher George Santayana once said, "Those who cannot remember the past are condemned to repeat it." On a personal level that axiom could be restated this way: "Those who don't pay attention to what got them into trouble yesterday are liable to end up in the same trouble tomorrow."

It's not very catchy, but you get the point.

We have about a zillion singles in our church. Many come to faith as a result of the brokenness associated with unsuccessful relationships. In his or her own way, each of these people comes asking the question, "Why does every relationship end the same way?" In most cases the answer is, "Because every relationship started the same way."

Not only did the relationships start the same way, they were conducted the same way as well. So, consequently, they all ended the same way. We mistakenly think that swapping partners will itself guarantee a different kind of relationship. It's the same line of thinking that leads us to buy new tennis rackets, golf clubs, and baseball bats—as if new equipment will somehow compensate for a poor swing. Expensive cookware does not necessarily result in gourmet cooking. A new guitar does not guarantee better music. And bad relational habits are not corrected by starting a new relationship.

So our question needs to be asked with an eye to the rearview mirror: *In light of your past experience, what is the wise thing to do?*

History Lessons

Your personal history is unique to you. And the sum of your past experiences predisposes you toward specific weaknesses and strengths in your relationships, finances, career, etc. For example, your personal history makes you more prone to temptation in some areas than in others. Consequently, what's safe for some folks may not be safe for you. There are activities that others find it easy to walk away from while you are prone to overindulge. So every decision, invitation, and opportunity that comes your way needs to be filtered through this question: In light of my past experience, what's the wise thing to do?

I have a friend who received some startling advice when he went through premarital counseling with his fiancée. The counselor told him, "You come from such a dysfunctional family that, when you return from your honeymoon, you need to come back in to see me."

My friend was shocked. The counselor continued, "We need

to spend about six months just working through the stuff you're bringing into this relationship. It isn't marriage problems I'm concerned about; it's the *you* problems that will impact the marriage."

Now, most people don't continue premarital counseling after the wedding. Most couples don't get *any* counseling before they say "I do." So my buddy had every right to ask Dr. Encouragement how often he required postnuptial visits from his premarital counselees and take his cue from there. But instead, a month after returning from his honeymoon, my friend went back for another round of counseling. Why? Not because it was standard operating procedure. Not because of a verse of Scripture. Not because of a universal moral or ethical imperative. He went back because, in light of his past experience, it was the *wise thing* for him to do.

It was a decision my friend never regretted. And it spoke volumes to his new wife about his commitment to their marriage.

Your past experience must be a grid through which you evaluate every decision. Chances are, there are places you have no business visiting because of your history—places that would have no impact on the average person, but the average person doesn't share your experience with those environments. Perhaps there are certain types of people you have no business spending time with. Being around them triggers something unhealthy in you.

I know people who refuse to buy on credit because of their past experience with credit cards. Is there anything inherently wrong with a credit card? I hope not. I use one all the time. But for those people whose pasts are cluttered with financial problems due to their unwise use of credit, it is wise to stay away.

I know guys who got rid of their satellite dishes. Women who canceled their Internet connections. Singles who quit dating for a season. All because of this important question.

These are men and women who had the courage to face up to God's will for their lives. They knew that their pasts set them up for failure if they did not take drastic steps. So in light of their past experience, they did the wise thing. The unusual thing. The extreme thing.

Gut Check

What about you? In light of your past experience, what is the wise thing for *you* to do?

What is the wise thing for you to do financially?

Professionally?

Relationally?

Where are you set up to fail because of something in your past? Perhaps it was something you had no control over, yet there it is, reaching into your current experience and wreaking havoc with your choices. Does the way you were raised predispose you to an area of temptation to which most people seem immune? If so, admit it. Own up to it. Don't be content with merely doing the right thing. *Do the wise thing.*

Seasonal Wisdom

Biding Your Time

I've suggested that asking our question from three different perspectives will provide you with a point of reference, giving you valuable insight into where you are and where you are headed. Here's the second form of the question.

In light of my current circumstances, what is the wise thing to do?

Life is seasonal. Today's sorrow will be replaced by tomorrow's joy. Today's anger will probably be tempered with tomorrow's perspective. Today's worry will be replaced by tomorrow's concerns. As Jesus taught, each day has its own worries. If we are not careful, we will allow the pressures, fears, and circumstances of today to drive us to make decisions we will regret tomorrow.

That being the case, you owe it to yourself and to the people you love to take your current emotions and state of mind into account when making decisions. I don't know about you, but most of my apologies stem from my propensity to react to the moment. When the moment has passed, I discover I have overreacted and hurt someone in the process. I can't begin to remember all the e-mails I wish I could *unsend*—I know that if I had waited even twenty-four hours, my responses would have been much different. Consequently, there would have been far less residual damage. When I'm mad, I've learned that the wise thing for me to do is *nothing*. Just wait.

Beyond the Moment

But this angle on our question goes beyond the moment. What's wise in this season of life may be unwise in the next. And vice versa.

For example, I have no problem with women working outside the home. Our church would cease to function without our incredible female staff. But for some women, during certain stages of their lives, maintaining a career outside the home is not the most prudent thing to do. The question is not, "Should women work outside the home?" Neither is it, "Should a particular woman work outside the home?" The question marketplace moms should ask is, "Is it wise for me to work outside the home during this particular season of life?"

Sandra sold real estate during the first four years of our marriage. When we had our first child, she came home to be a full-time mom. That was an easy decision. A few years later, as our children got older, there were times we toyed with the idea of her jumping back into the workforce. This was especially enticing when someone asked her to help list or find an expensive (read: high-commission) home.

But for us, it always came back to our question. Whereas it might have been financially profitable for Sandra to jump back into real estate, in light of that season of life, it wouldn't have been the wise thing to do.

No Decision

Every pastor is forced to grapple with issues surrounding divorce and remarriage. I am certainly not immune. As I mentioned, we have several thousand singles in our church, many of them nursing the wounds from painful divorces. At the same time, these hurting people desire companionship. And more often than not, before the ink is dry on the divorce papers, they are already in new relationships. And those who aren't in one are looking for one. I imagine I would be the same way.

Now, there's nothing wrong with desiring companionship. There's nothing wrong with moving on with your life once you have closed the door on a difficult chapter. But those aren't really the issues. For single men and women who find themselves in this challenging season of life, the question they must ask is, "In light of what I've just come through, my current state of mind, my frazzled emotions, what is the wise thing to do relationally?"

Dozens of times newly divorced men and women have asked me what I think about remarriage. I give people the same advice. I tell them to pull out their calendars and mark the day one year from today. Then I tell them not to make any decisions or even form an opinion about remarriage for a year. Why? Because in light of their current reality, it is usually unwise to try to make that kind of decision. Some people take my advice, and of those, many have written to thank me. Most people think I'm too extreme. Some of them have had the courage to write and tell me they wish they had listened. A handful of people actually make appointments to come in with their new spouses and get advice about how to rescue their second marriages. I never say, "I told you so." But I certainly think it.

I feel so strongly about this that I have asked our pastors not to perform second marriages for individuals who have been divorced for less than two years. Do I have a verse to support this policy? Nope. Is it wrong to remarry before two years have passed? That's not the issue. It all goes back to our question: What is the wise thing to do? I've never heard anyone attribute their marriage problems to the fact that they waited too long to marry. But I've talked to countless folks who wish they had waited longer.

Look Around

So in light of what's going on in your life right now, what is the wise thing for you to do? As you consider your frame of mind, your emotional state, and even your physical health, what is the wise thing to do? As you consider your current responsibilities and commitments, things that a year from now may not be a factor, what is the wise thing to do? As you examine the status of your finances, what is the wise thing to do?

Again, life is seasonal. What is appropriate today may be completely inappropriate a month from now. What is foolish today may be prudent tomorrow. It is not enough to determine what is legal, permissible, or even practical. As a Christ follower, you have been called to approach life with a different standard. So you must ask, "For me, in light of my past experience and my current season of life, what is the wise thing to do?"

Looking Ahead

Creating a Preferred Future

O ur question will provide you with the greatest insight when asked from three different angles. Again, each form of the question will provide you with a unique perspective on your options and decisions. Here's the final version of the question:

In light of my future hopes and dreams, what is the wise thing to do?

No doubt, you have a mental picture of how you want your future to look. It may be general. It may be scripted out in detail. You may have gone to the effort of writing it down, complete with incremental steps and artificial deadlines. While certain personalities are driven to slave over their goals and objectives, others are content to simply dream. Either way, we all have mental pictures of how we want our futures to pan out—a mental image of what could and should be.

If I were to ask you where you envision yourself in ten years financially, you could come up with an answer. You have some idea of what that should look like. You may not have a plan for getting there, but you almost certainly have a mental picture of what you would like the future to look like financially. If you were pressed to describe your future relationally or professionally, you could come up with a general description for those aspects of your life as well. We all have certain hopes and dreams for the future. We may lack plans, but we certainly have dreams and expectations.

Dream Wreckers

The truth is, most people's dreams don't come true. I don't know too many adults who are living their dreams. And while it is true that the twists and turns of life can reshape our futures, that is not the primary reason people are robbed of their dreams. We rob ourselves. We rob ourselves when we make decisions in the moment with no thought of how those decisions will impact our futures.

This is easy to see in others. But somehow, the man or woman in the mirror is always the exception, or so we think.

You know people who have robbed themselves of their preferred futures. Too much debt, too much alcohol, too many risks, too many relationships, too many nights out, too many missed classes. We have all watched somebody we care about trade his or her dreams for a moment, a weekend, a habit, a promise, or a kiss.

As a parent, I constantly urged my kids to make today's decisions in light of tomorrow's hopes and dreams. The future is what brings today's choices into proper focus. Making choices with the end in mind goes a long way toward ensuring a happy ending.

Today's decisions must be evaluated in light of how they will impact and shape tomorrow. Short of winning the lottery, your financial future will be determined by today's financial decisions. The health of your marriage tomorrow will be determined by the decisions you make today. The nature of my relationship with my children now that they are grown has hinged, in large part, on the decisions I made while they were younger and at home.

I was reminded of the significance of this principle one day as I listened to a brokenhearted father describe his failed attempts to reconnect with his adult daughter. He could not understand why she refused to return his calls or accept his gifts. She was now married and had a little girl of her own. In her father's words, she was "depriving him" of his right to be the grandfather he had always dreamed of being. From where he stood, she had shut him out of her life for good, and with no justification. He was devastated.

But that wasn't the whole story.

When his daughter turned twelve, this man was in the third year of an affair with an employee. His wife knew what was going on but could never prove it. On many occasions, she would drive around their small town, looking for his car. Their daughter was with her mom the night she spotted his car in a hotel parking lot at the edge of town. This twelve-year-old girl saw her father come out of the room with his girlfriend in tow. She endured the humiliation that accompanied the divorce proceedings. And then she didn't hear from her father for fifteen years.

As much as I empathized with a father who wanted a relationship with his only daughter, I couldn't help but think, *You did this to yourself. You robbed yourself of the joy of seeing your daughter graduate from high school. You missed the once-in-a-lifetime opportunity to give her away at her wedding. You weren't there for the birth of your granddaughter.* One stupid, irresponsible decision robbed him of what could have been and what should have been.

But he wasn't the only person whose dreams wouldn't come true. His daughter certainly didn't imagine growing up without her father. His wife certainly didn't dream of becoming a single mom. His decision derailed the dreams of everyone who was close to him. The shrapnel of his choices wounded everyone who loved him. In a moment, the future was changed forever. Nobody's dreams would come true.

Future Tense, Common Sense

Asking our question with the future in mind casts a trenchant light on the validity of our options. The deceptive shades of gray dissipate. The nature of the journey on which we are about to embark becomes painfully clear. So clear that we are tempted to look away, to retreat to the often-rehearsed excuses that have buttressed our misguided decisions for years: *I'm not doing anything wrong. People do it all the time. I'm not hurting anyone. I can handle it. There's no law against it. Nobody's going to find out. Nothing's going to happen.*

The director of our student ministry once asked each of our high school students to write a letter to his or her future spouse. The response was amazing. For most of the students, this was the first time they had given their undivided attention to what they were looking forward to relationally. In a defining moment, it dawned on these young people how their current behavior would be either an investment in or a deterrent to that future relationship.

Following the letter-writing exercise, the leaders enacted a mock wedding, and our students were transported to an event so far in the future that it seemed to have no connection to the realities of their everyday lives. But in that moment, when they were fast-forwarded to a marriage altar with all it represents, the casual decisions of adolescence took on extraordinary meaning. Suddenly, they realized that their tomorrows would, in fact, be shaped by today. The decisions made at thirteen would sculpt what life looked like at thirty-one.

The students were not the only ones moved by this exercise. Our adult leaders were impacted as well. But as you can imagine, their takeaway was somewhat different from that of the students. Their response: "I wish someone had helped me to stop and think about my decisions based on how they would affect me in the future." Most of us had someone in our lives who tried. But we were seventeen and knew everything.

The fact that the adults would feel that way should tell you something very important about all of us: our lives would be better today if along the way we'd been asking our question. We might be closer to living our dreams if we had guarded them more closely.

Is it too late to begin viewing today through the lens of tomorrow? I don't think so. Chances are, you've got plenty of tomorrows left.

So that settles it, right? From now on you will gauge the appropriateness of every option by your hopes and dreams for tomorrow. Every time there is a decision to make, you will reflexively stop and ask, "In light of my future hopes and dreams, what is the wise thing to do?" And then you will do it!

End of story. No need to finish this book.

Maybe Not

It's not that simple, is it? Or is it? Seems strange that we would digest this information and then turn right around and resist the obvious.

Isn't it ironic that at this very moment you are seriously contemplating a decision that has the potential to chip away at your preferred future, and yet you are leaning hard in that direction, rehearsing the same old worn-out excuses? You know which ones I'm talking about. The ones you've been using since high school. The ones that cleared the way for you to do things you now wish you hadn't. Things you have never shared with your spouse. Things you hope your children never discover. Decisions you are ashamed of...choices that, to this day, cast a shadow over the good things that have come your way. Options that, if avoided, would have paved the way for your dreams to come true.

Sorry to be so hard on you. It's just that I know my own tendency to deny this truth in the face of overwhelming evidence to the contrary. As I said earlier, it's easy to see how this principle has played out in the lives of others while ignoring its relevance in our own lives. We are a people proficient in the art of self-deception.

So let's get specific. In light of where you want to be financially in ten years, what's the wise thing to do right now? What do you need to start or stop doing financially?

If you are single, in hopes of one day finding the man or woman of your dreams, what is the wise way to conduct your relationships now? What are you doing that has the potential to rob you of your preferred future? What do you want to tell your future spouse about your past relationships? Live accordingly. If you are married and your dream is to finish life together with your spouse, what options do you need to take off the table? What's out there that could steal your dream? What precautions need to be taken? What's the wise thing to do relationally?

In light of how you envision your relationship with your children when they're teenagers or in college or married with children of their own, what is the wise thing to do now? What practices would you be wise to incorporate now into your parenting repertoire? Where do you need to reprioritize?

It would be nice if we could go back and redo adolescence. Oh, and maybe drop in and redo some chapters from our twenties and thirties. But, of course, we can't. We only get one shot at every season of life. Whether or not we learned anything becomes evident in the seasons that follow.

So what have you learned? More to the point, are you willing to face up to God's will for your life? Are you ready to acknowledge what you know in your heart is true? Are you prepared to ask our question and then to follow through? Take a giant step toward protecting your future. *In light of your future hopes and dreams, what is the wise thing to do?*

Where Does It Hurt?

For just a moment, let's pretend that no one, including God, can read your mind. Better yet, let's imagine that five minutes from now you will be able to erase your next five minutes' worth of thoughts. In other words, let's create some space for unfiltered thinking. You will not be accountable to anyone, including yourself, for the thoughts you are about to entertain.

If you can go with this for just a minute, you will be free to admit to yourself anything you want without feeling like you have to do anything about it. Because in five minutes, you will be able to erase any incriminating thoughts that you allow yourself to think. Are you with me?

Okay, let's do a little probing. Remember, you are free to admit to yourself anything you want. No action will be required.

As you evaluate where you are financially, relationally, morally, professionally, and spiritually, what would you do differently in each of these areas if you were to embrace our question? In light of your past experience, current circumstances, and future hopes and dreams, what is the wise thing to do financially? Relationally? Morally? Professionally? Spiritually?

Again, you don't have to act on your answers. Just take a moment to be painfully honest with yourself. What would you do differently in each of these areas if you were to evaluate each component of your life through the lens of this question?

Remember, you're not asking this question for anybody but yourself. What's the wise thing *for me* to do? Resist the temptation to hide behind broad generalities and cultural norms. What is the wise thing for *you* to do? You are a unique blend of past experiences, current circumstances, and future hopes and dreams.

Wisdom allows you to customize the decision-making process to your specific professional, financial, and relational dimensions. Don't miss this opportunity.

Think about how different your life would be now if you had been processing your options this way from the beginning. Imagine how different your life might look a year from now if you embraced our question from this point forward.

Okay, back to the real world. No need to feel guilty about what you just admitted to yourself but don't intend to do anything about. We've got several more chapters to wear down your resistance.

Part 2

The Alternatives

Opting Out

The Way of the Not-So-Wise

That last exercise hurt a little, huh? I'm sorry. But look, we all know that sometimes a little pain is good. Actually, maybe it didn't hurt so much as make you sad. You sure wish you could go back and do things differently. But what comes next could help moving forward. Because what I'm asking you to do now is to just start practicing asking yourself that question: *If I were a wise man or wise woman, in light of my past experience, my current circumstances, and my future hopes and dreams, what's the wise thing to do?*

I'm asking you to do this because you owe it to yourself to at least be aware of the answer. That's all we're aiming for at this point—self-awareness. You see, asking that question and recognizing an answer will probably lead to a string of thoughts. You may find yourself thinking, *I can see the wise thing to do here, but I don't want to do it.* That's a huge step forward in self-awareness.

You've just learned something extremely valuable about yourself. The insight you just gained might even be this: *I don't have my own best interests in mind.* If that's the case, you definitely want to know it.

This will likely trigger more questions: *If I don't have my best interests in mind, who does? And where's that going to lead?* But, like I said, just start getting in the habit throughout your day, decision by decision, of calling our question to mind: *What's the wise thing for me to do here?*

The Wise and the Not-So-Wise

There's one person in the Bible that we don't have to wonder *if* about; he was a wise man, said to be the wisest man who ever lived, so much so that he wrote the Bible's book of Proverbs. His name was Solomon, a name that even sounds wise, huh? In the pages of Proverbs, King Solomon portrayed four different kinds of people. Foremost among them, he said, are the wise, the people who look at the past, the present, and the future and make the best decisions.

But wise man that he was, Solomon didn't stop there. He also described three other categories, three alternatives to being wise and living wisely. Solomon's proverb is showing us that when we walk *away* from wisdom, we walk *toward* something else. If we don't intentionally opt for wisdom, then we accidentally opt for one of those other three things. It's as if Solomon was saying, "As you're learning what wisdom looks like, let me also show you what it clearly doesn't look like."

So let's take a close look at *the unwise*. But I may as well warn you; what Solomon said here, what we're about to explore, is offensive. It just might make you angry. So bear with me and be willing at least to listen as Solomon speaks to us across the centuries. You owe it to yourself.

The Simple

Let's start with the character Solomon described as *simple*. The reason such people are unwise is *not* that they're against wisdom, but that they just haven't lived long enough to know better. They're simply too young. The *simple* are the naive, the clueless. They're not bad; they're not evil; they're not dumb. They're not trying to ruin their lives. They just lack something older people have: *experience.*

Solomon tells us a fascinating story, beginning in Proverbs 7:6, about a young man convinced he's heading for a good time. But as we read about his situation, that ominous music from *Jaws* starts playing in the background. With each step he takes, you want to reach out, grab his arm, and yell *Stop!* Solomon described him as "like an ox going to the slaughter, like a deer stepping into a noose…like a bird darting into a snare, little knowing it will cost him his life" (7:22–23).

Being young and youthful is a beautiful experience. It can also be a dangerous experience because, well, you're young and youthful. And your tendency, when someone a little older tries to warn you of dangers ahead, is to say, "Nah, I've got this. Nothing's gonna happen!" But Solomon shows us that actually a lot can happen and your life can change tracks in a click. And suddenly you find yourself traveling in a direction you never in your simple mind intended.

I realize this sounds like Solomon and I are Debby Downers on being young. We're not. If you're young, here's the amazing thing. Even though you lack experience, you have an opportunity the rest of us can only wish for, an advantage we'd love to have. You can enjoy the benefits of youth *and* the benefits of wisdom, all at the same time. The fact that you're simple and a bit clueless and naive (I warned you, this is offensive) does not have to derail your life. You do *not* have to learn everything the hard way.

You can have both. You can have your youth, and you can have wisdom. But you'll have to *seek* wisdom. It won't come naturally. You'll have to *ask* for it, and you'll have to learn to ask. It's a practice, a process. You'll have to stop and think at every invitation, every opportunity, every decision, *Okay, if I was a wise young man or woman, what would be the wise thing for me to do? In light*

of my past experience (which isn't much)...in light of my current cir-
cumstances (yes it's true, I'm very young)...and in light of my future
hopes and dreams (which mean so much to me)...

The Fool

Our wise man Solomon apparently valued candor. He didn't pull
any punches. He called his next character a fool. The difference
between the simple person and the fool is that the fool *knows* his
choices are unwise. He knows from experience. But the fool just
doesn't care. He doesn't give a _____ (fill in the blank with
whatever word you *wisely* think he'd use). He might also add, "It's
my life, and it's none of your _____ business."

Proverbs gives us a visual for the fool that's just hard to get out
of your head: "As a dog returns to its vomit, so fools repeat their
folly" (Proverbs 26:11). I told you, he doesn't pull punches. If
there's an area in your life where you tell yourself, "I know this is
wrong, but I'm going to do it anyway, and probably repeat it,"
Solomon would answer, "In that area of your life, you're a fool."

And while time is the cure for the simple person, the cure for
the fool isn't so easy. The fool has to learn the hard way. The cure
is always tragedy. And like all tragedies, it never happens in a
vacuum. The fool keeps saying, "It's my life, I can do what I want.
It's *my* body, *my* time, *my* money, and this doesn't affect other
people. *I'm not hurting anyone.*" Sounds like a fool, huh?

His foolishness has blinded him to his selfishness. Solomon said it well, "A companion of fools suffers harm" (Proverbs 13:20). The fool's companion—the spouse, the parents, the brother or sister, the employee, the children, the friend—cannot escape harm from the fool's wrong choices. The tragedy of being a fool is that eventually you'll inflict harm upon someone else. There's always collateral damage. And while the fool may protest all day long, "Well, that wasn't my intention," the reality is, *No, but you've still hurt that person.*

The Mocker

In a sense, Solomon is giving us the good *(the simple),* the bad *(the fool),* and the ugly *(the mocker).* And this last category is really ugly.

The *mocker*—or in some translations, the *scoffer*—is the fool on steroids. It's the man or woman who not only doesn't care about the difference between right and wrong, wise and unwise, but is also constantly mocking or scoffing at other people who pursue what's right and what's wise.

Mockers are cynical, critical, condescending, and controlling. You always feel off balance around them. You never know where you stand. They always try to come across as the smartest person in the room, and they use that supposed knowledge to try to dominate and manipulate their world and their relationships.

Look, if you're married to somebody like this, or you work for somebody like this, I'm very sorry. Because Solomon said, "Whoever corrects a mocker invites insults; whoever rebukes the wicked incurs abuse. Do not rebuke mockers or they will hate you" (Proverbs 9:7–8). Bottom line? You can't win with them. They just don't listen. They leverage whatever intellect they think they have, and they pounce on you. Whether it's their insecurity or just pure arrogance or something from their past, they just have to control the situation through their cynicism and criticism. They're almost impossible to have a relationship with. They're unwise, and often border on inhuman.

So there you go: the wise and the unwise as presented by the always-wise Solomon. If you recognized one or more of your past choices as belonging in one of the not-so-wise categories, you've gained an additional level of self-awareness, perhaps enough to consider heading in a different direction. If so, that's where your new habit comes into play: watching yourself in each and every situation and asking, "What is the wise thing to do?"

At some point in their lives, the simple, the fool, and even the mocker will sense the need for help in decision making. They'll know they need *wisdom*. But the larger question then is, *Will they even be able to recognize it?* Will you?

Turn Around

180 Degrees Toward Hope

Remember that point I raised in the conclusion of the last chapter about not being able to recognize the need for wisdom? It has to be raised because it's part of the hard work of asking the vital question, *What's the wise thing to do?* The problem, as we learn from Solomon, is that you can get stuck in one of those unwise categories for so long that you risk becoming a person who "seeks wisdom and finds none" (Proverbs 14:6). At that point you've done permanent damage to your life, your relationships, and, in some cases, your soul. You've become a person who cannot receive correction. Instead of becoming as hard as nails (sometimes necessary in this life), you've become a nail (usually only responsive to the blunt force of a hammer). That kind of situation is almost hopeless.

Almost.

Come and Get It

I find it interesting that at the very beginning of the book of Proverbs, Solomon pictures wisdom as a woman who's walking through the streets of a town calling out, "Who wants wisdom? Come and get it!" It's tempting to jump ahead here, but you really need to meet this woman:

> Out in the open wisdom calls aloud, she raises her voice in
> the public square; on top of the wall she cries out, at the
> city gate she makes her speech: "How long will you who
> are simple love your simple ways? How long will mockers
> delight in mockery and fools hate knowledge?" (1:20–22)

Two words are at the heart of this speech: *How long?* But those two words pulse out into a phrase we all know too well: *Aren't you tired?* Ask anybody these days how he's doing, and you're almost sure to get a common response: *I'm tired.* Many of us have something in our lives that has just gone on too long. We're ready for some relief, but we're not sure things can change.

Into this scenario "Wisdom" comes walking down the street and addresses the simple: "Aren't you tired of learning everything the hard way?" Then she addresses the mocker: "Aren't you tired of yet another failed relationship with someone you care for?" Then the fool: "Aren't you tired of another year looking just like the year before with the same problems, same hang-ups, same dashed hopes?" Again, this feels almost hopeless.

Almost.

Listen as Wisdom declares what must be done:

Repent at my rebuke! Then I will pour out my thoughts to you, I will make known to you my teachings. (1:23)

Repent. Turn from going one direction and go in another. That's where the hope lies, in the turning. But as you can see, it's an active hope; there's an action necessary for it to be realized.

But whoever listens to me will live in safety and be at ease, without fear of harm. (1:33)

"Come on," Wisdom says, "I'm giving you one more opportunity. I'm giving you one more chance. I'm calling, calling, calling...*Listen to me!* And whoever hears me will find the good way of security and peace and protection. There's still hope."

So you see, that's why we ask the question: *In light of my past experience, in light of my current circumstances, in light of my future hopes and dreams—regardless of where that leads—if I was wise, what would I do?*

If you're a mocker, you have to start admitting you're not the smartest person in the room.

If you're a fool, you've got to start caring, because it's not just about you. It's about everybody who loves you and depends on you.

If you're young and simple—and there's nothing wrong with that—you have the opportunity of a lifetime. You can have both. You can have both youth and wisdom, but you won't get there by yourself. You've got to ask for it. Wisdom is available. It's there for us.

But here's the reality. And it breaks my heart when I see it or hear it, which happens all too often. Sometimes people stay away from wisdom for so long that when they finally decide they want to fix their lives, they can't. Some things are too broken to be repaired in this life, and I emphasize *in this life*. God will restore all things, make all things new in his time, but you may never have the relationship with your wife you wanted. You may never see that dream come to pass. You may not get what you want, not in this life.

You reap what you sow. I reap what I sow. But wisdom is just as crucial for facing the consequences of your past life as it is for taking the next step or steps into the future. Our same question still applies though: *What's the wise thing for me to do?* The answer in this case will be hopeful, but it will be a hope colored by scars and tears, a hope that's weathered.

But that doesn't make it any less a hope.

And there's no better time to move toward hope, toward wisdom, than now, especially in the two areas we turn our attention to next.

Part 3

A Question of Time

Time Bandits

Having the Time of Your Life

When it comes to asking our question, there is no more crucial arena than that of *time*. Your time equals your life. You can run out of money and still have some life left. You can run out of friends with life to spare. But once you run out of time, it's over.

If there is one commodity we must learn to handle wisely, it is our time. Think about it. You can make more money, make new friends, take more trips, maybe even have another child. But your allotment of time is inflexible. You only get so much of it. Job put it this way:

> A person's days are determined; you have decreed the
> number of his months and have set limits he cannot
> exceed. (Job 14:5)

Did you catch those last four words? "Limits he cannot exceed." You can overspend, overeat, and overachieve, but you can't "overlive."

The psalmist adds this insight regarding the relationship between our allotment of time and wisdom:

Teach us to number our days, that we may gain a heart of wisdom. (Psalm 90:12)

I love that verse. Simply by recognizing that our days are numbered, we take a giant step toward becoming men and women of wisdom.

Just the sheer recognition that our time on this earth is limited should compel us to evaluate all of life differently. Unfortunately, we spend more of our lives asking for the time than evaluating how well we're investing it. But as we are about to discover, there's something far more significant than knowing what time it is: it's knowing what to do with our time.

Which Way Did It Go?

Sandra and I were married for almost five years before we had our first child. When we think back to those days of child-free living, we often wonder, *What in the world did we do with all that extra time?* Shouldn't we have something significant to show for those unencumbered years? Where did all that time go?

The answer: away.

It went *away.* And there is no way to recover a minute of it. There is no leftover time. It can't be saved up for later. You can't store it. It just goes away. So we all look back and wonder where the time went. It seems like just yesterday I was sixteen. Where did my twenties go? Why don't I have more to show for my thirties?

When we ask, "Where did the time go?" we are really asking another, more bewildering, question: "Where did my *life* go?" You see, what we do with our time is more important than simply knowing what time it is, how old we are, or even how much time we have left. The fact that time is life and can't be recovered is why we must place this priceless commodity under the scrutiny of our much bigger question:

In light of my past experience, my current responsibilities, and my future hopes and dreams, what is the wisest way to invest my time?

Now, we could end this chapter right here. You are smart enough to objectively evaluate your time commitments and make the necessary adjustments. And you have lived long enough to know that time is life. But before we move on, I would like to dig deeper into one aspect of time that so often eludes us. This is something everybody figures out eventually, but sometimes *eventually* is too late. This is one of those life lessons that, regardless of when we learn it, we wish we had learned it earlier.

Chipping Away

I will keep this simple because this is actually a very simple principle. I've broken it down into five statements. Here's the first:

1. There is a cumulative value to investing small amounts of time in certain activities over a long period.

Exercise is an obvious illustration of this principle. There's a clear cumulative effect from exercising a few minutes every day or every other day over a long period. At the end of a year, you can see and feel a difference. But at the end of your first exercise session, the only difference is that you are sore. You will see almost no measurable benefit from one exercise session; in fact, no matter how long you have been exercising, there is almost no measurable benefit from a single session. That's why it is so easy to talk yourself out of exercising. *What will it hurt if I miss one day?* The answer is, it won't hurt anything, physically speaking. The real value in exercise is not found in any one deposit of time; the value is realized at the end of a sequence of deposits. Exercise has a compounding effect. The consistent, incremental investment of time makes a difference.

The same is true if you are attempting to master a musical instrument or perfect your golf swing or gain proficiency in the martial arts. A little bit of concentrated effort several days a week over a period of six months will drastically improve your performance.

Now, what is obviously true in the realms of physical fitness and music is not so obvious in other areas. Nevertheless, it has implications for just about every facet of our lives, especially those pertaining to relationships. Let me list a few specific practices where consistency will make a difference: dinner with the family, date night with your spouse, time alone with God, church attendance, one-on-one time with your children, praying with your family, small-group Bible study, going to bed at the same time as your spouse.

There is no real measurable gain derived from any of these activities if you are keeping score based solely on any individual installment of time. What's the takeaway from putting your kids to bed one Tuesday night? Occasionally, you might have a significant conversation with one of your children. Or a single evening of Bible study with a small group? On a good night, you might gain a new insight from someone in your small group. But for the most part, it wouldn't be the end of the world if you did something else with that time. Dinner with the family is, well, it is dinner with the family. What is gained in one installment of time around the dinner table? Not much.

But as a father who kept the habit of eating dinner with his family five or six nights a week, I can tell you that there is cumulative value in that seemingly unimportant routine. As a Christian who was taught early on to open God's Word alone every morning, I can vouch for the cumulative value of those incremental investments of time. And as a couple that has devoted three Monday nights a month to participating in a small group, Sandra and I know the cumulative value of being in community with a handful of other believers.

No specific dinnertime conversation comes to mind. I can't think of a particular discussion with our small group that changed my life. Bedtime conversations with my children are rarely all that productive or memorable. But these routines, these incremental investments of time—life—have immeasurable cumulative value.

And that leads me to my second statement:

2. There are rarely immediate consequences for neglecting single installments of time in any arena of life.

Once again, it is in the realm of our health that we find the clearest example of this maxim. Neglect your health for a day and there are no immediate consequences. Neglect your health for a week and you won't experience any negative effects. In fact, after a week of fast food, double desserts, no exercise, a few too many beers, and several late nights out on the town, you may wonder why you didn't adopt this lifestyle earlier. (Or you may wonder why you gave it up!) If you were to evaluate the effects of such a lifestyle after a single week, you would probably draw some wrong conclusions. Other than a little indigestion and some difficulty getting up in the mornings, there wouldn't seem to be anything to worry about.

This same dynamic plays itself out in every area of life. If you miss dinner with the family one night, it's no big deal. If you choose to sleep in one Sunday morning, nothing changes. Skip work one Friday and you'll probably still have a job on Monday. Pick up a newspaper instead of your Bible one morning and life goes on. It's deceiving but true that we rarely see any immediate consequences for neglecting a single installment of time in any arena of life. But if neglect becomes your pattern, you will eventually bump up against our third principle:

3. Neglect has a cumulative effect.

You can neglect your health for a week or maybe even a month without any serious consequences. But strap that lifestyle on for ten or twelve years and the damage might be irreversible. Not because of a single night out or one particular meal. The effect is cumulative.

Neglect has a cumulative effect physically, relationally, spiritually, professionally, financially, emotionally, and horticulturally.

Horticulturally? I just looked out at my lawn. Neglect anything over a long period and you will have something to show for it. Usually a mess—a mess that can generate a wave of concern and even energy. Suddenly we realize what we have done, and we rush out to the yard to reverse the consequences of our neglect.

But in the areas that matter most, a burst of energy and activity cannot reverse the consequences that accompany a season of neglect. More on that a little later.

The next stop in our five-point journey is something you have probably never thought about but have certainly experienced. While it is true that small, consistent investments of time add up to good things and that consistent neglect adds up to bad things, the random pursuits that we allow to interrupt our important routines add up to *no-thing:*

4. There is no cumulative value to the urgent things we allow to interfere with the important things.

Allow me to illustrate. Let's suppose your New Year's resolution this past January was to exercise three days a week. You joined a health club. You bought a treadmill. You announced to friends and family that this would be your year to get in shape. Now let's imagine that it hasn't worked out. Other things kept interfering with your exercise routine. Chances are, you do not have to use much imagination on this one, but let's take it a step further.

Now imagine that you have to sit down with a friend six

months into the year and explain what you did instead of exercising. How might that conversation go?

"What did you do instead of exercising?" she asks.

"Um, I don't know. A lot of things, I guess."

"Well, let's think about it. Did you sleep in a few mornings?"

"Yeah, that's right. Sometimes I got a few extra hours of sleep."

"Okay, how many times?"

"I don't know."

"What else did you do instead of exercising?"

"I went to the office early."

"How many times?"

"I don't know."

"What did you do at the office?"

"Different stuff."

"What stuff?"

"I can't remember. Just stuff. Work stuff."

"Okay. What else did you do with those mornings instead of exercise?

"On a couple of occasions, I had breakfast with friends."

"What else?"

"Some mornings I just got up and piddled around the house. Checked my e-mail. Helped get the kids off to school."

Here's the point: If you stack up all the stuff you did instead of exercising, then added up their value, what would you end up with? Zero. The random pursuits that interrupt our important routines don't add up to anything. Well, actually, they add up to a lot of wasted time. There's never any cumulative value to all the things we do *instead of* the things we know are truly important.

What's the cumulative value of all the things a college freshman does instead of studying? Zero. What's the cumulative value of all the things a father does instead of having dinner with his family? Zero. What's the cumulative value of all the things that have interfered with your devotional time? Zero.

When random urgent activities constantly interfere with strategic deposits of time, it is like throwing away our most precious commodity. It is worse than wasting time. We waste our lives.

This principle explains why we don't have more to show for our time. It all gets gobbled up with random, unquantifiable activities—activities that rob us of what's most important. When you add up all the what-I-did-instead-ofs, they always equal zero.

Before we dive into the fifth and final statement, let's look at what we have said so far.

- There is a cumulative value to investing small amounts of time in certain activities over a long period.
- There are rarely any immediate consequences for neglecting single installments of time in any arena of life.
- Neglect has a cumulative effect.

- There is no cumulative value to the urgent things we allow to interfere with the important things.

If all of this is true, and time equals life, what is the wise thing to do as it relates to your time?

My fifth point is so important I'm dedicating the entire next chapter to it.

Live and Learn

Eddie Money Was Right

Surely you remember Eddie Money. Big pop star in the 1980s. Lots of hits. Very cool-looking guy. He usually appeared in still photos with a cigarette perched between his fingers. The reason I bring him up is that one of his biggest hits underscores the searing truth of our fifth and final statement about time. The song is titled "I Wanna Go Back." The chorus goes like this:

> I want go back and do it all over again,
> but I can't go back, I know.

Eddie's right. We can't go back. We can't go back and relive, relove, retrieve, rearrange, reprioritize, redirect, or refocus. Looking back, there are times we wanna go back. But we can't. You can't relive your teens, twenties, or thirties. You can't rewind your marriage. You can't raise your kids again. Depressed yet?

Here's my fifth and final statement concerning my principle for using time wisely:

5. In the critical arenas of life, you cannot make up for lost time.

As students, we could pull all-nighters to make up for the studying we should have been doing all week. On vacation you can drive a little faster than normal to make up the time lost during your four-year-old's potty breaks. But in the world of relationships, there are no all-nighters. You can't cram for a better relationship with your kids or your spouse. Speeding up doesn't make up for lost time with your heavenly Father. The important areas of life require small deposits *all along the way.* And if you miss those opportunities, they are lost forever.

Most of us have made the mistake of trying to make up for missed time in the gym. You know what I'm talking about. You haven't exercised in years; then suddenly you decide to get back into shape. So what do you do? The MEGA WORKOUT. You strap yourself into every machine in the building. You lift every weight. You log in time on the treadmill, the Lifecycle, the Stair-Master, the elliptical. You do it all. You know better, but something in you says, "I can make up for lost time; I can make up for my neglect." And so you walk away convinced that you have re-claimed lost ground. You feel so toned, so in shape. You even con-sider running for governor.

But the next morning you can't get out of bed. In fact, you are so sore you don't go to the gym for a week. Or worse, you injure yourself and are out for even longer. The moral of the story is, you cannot make up for lost time in the areas of life that matter most.

So what is the wise thing to do now?

Dad, it won't do any good to rush home tonight and an-nounce to the family, "It just occurred to me that I've missed too many dinners with the fam. So load up! Tonight, we're going to eat out at *all* our favorite restaurants. We'll go till midnight or later if we have to. We'll eat and eat and eat, and talk and talk and talk. We are making up for lost time."

Ridiculous? Perhaps. But no more ridiculous than thinking a long vacation can make up for being an absentee parent. It is no more ridiculous than promising a romantic weekend getaway to make up for months of work-related travel. A weekend together can't rescue a marriage that's been neglected for six months or more—no matter how romantic you make it.

Relationships are built on small, consistent deposits of time. You can't cram for what's most important. If you want to connect with your kids, you've got to be available consistently, not randomly. A vacation or weekend getaway is a good way to commemorate or celebrate the past or even changes on the horizon. But neither can compensate for consistent neglect.

So once again, what is the wise thing for you to do?

Redeeming the Time

With these five statements as a backdrop, look once again at Paul's warning to the believers in Ephesus:

> Be very careful, then, how you live—not as unwise but as wise, *making the most of every opportunity,* because the days are evil. (Ephesians 5:15–16)

The phrase "making the most of every opportunity" is often translated "making the most of your time"; it's literally "redeeming the time." The Greek term used here is an accounting term. Paul was saying, "Get the full value out of your time—squeeze all the good you can out of every moment of your life." Misappropriated time is misappropriated life. Be wise. Make the most of your time. You can't go back and reinvest it.

Did you catch the reason Paul gave for redeeming the time? "Because the days are evil."

As we said earlier, we don't live in a morally or ethically neutral environment. As a follower of Christ, your values are constantly being challenged—challenged by another value system. If you aren't on your guard, the culture will draw you into a lifestyle where your time is frivolously consumed rather than strategically invested. You will be busy. You may even be productive. But if you are not being "careful," you will miss those irretrievable opportunities to make small, incremental time deposits in the things that matter most. If you are not walking wisely, your time will be fragmented by a thousand urgent, disconnected opportunities and events. Such opportunities and events will seem important at the time, but when strung together they have no cumulative value.

But if you are willing to harness your time and appropriate it strategically, things can be different. You will be healthier physically, relationally, spiritually, and possibly, financially. You will look back at this next season of life with few, if any, regrets. Not because of a single day or a single burst of activity, but because of a single decision: the decision to get full value out of your time by making small, incremental investments of time in the things that matter most.

Studio Time Can Be Expensive

So in the light of your past, your present, and your future hopes and dreams, what needs to change about the way you are spending your time? What do you need to stop doing? What do you need to cancel? Chances are, the things that come to mind are not *bad* things. But remember, we have been called to a higher standard. What is the *wise* thing to do with your time? What in your current schedule is distracting you from making incremental investments of time in what's most important?

The biggest test I have ever faced in this area came two decades ago, right after Garrett, our second son, was born. I love music. In the early days of my marriage, I had a little music studio in our condo, along with a lot of gear that I had started accumulating when I was single. Marriage certainly cut into my studio time, but I continued to find a few hours here and there to disappear into my private world of music. When our first son, Andrew, was born, I found it increasingly difficult to carve out time for music. Sandra was very understanding and encouraged me to take whatever time I could find to pursue my musical interest.

Right after Garrett was born, we moved into a larger rental house. I was in the basement hooking up all my stuff one night when suddenly a thought hit me: *You know, Andy, you're about to invest another big block of your life in something that is fun but not very productive, and upstairs are the three people you love the most, and two of them are in diapers.* As I sat there thinking about the future, I knew that one day I would look back and wish I had invested more time with the people I loved and less time with the hobby I loved. I knew that the block of time—life—I would invest in music would be better spent with my family.

I went upstairs and announced to Sandra that I wasn't even

going to set my studio up, but instead I was going to sell everything. She was both shocked and relieved. In spite of her patience and encouragement, I knew there were times when she felt like she had to compete for my attention.

Looking back, that was one of the best decisions I ever made. There was nothing wrong with having a music studio, but in light of my desire to stay meaningfully connected to my family, giving it up was the wise thing for me to do. Do I miss my music? Sometimes. But I have never second-guessed my decision. And twenty years later, I am still enjoying the dividends from that simple decision. Besides, I can't imagine adding a time-consuming hobby to my already-packed schedule. But hey, that's just me. The question is, *What is the wise thing for you to do?*

I'm not suggesting that if you have a music studio, art studio, darkroom, shop, or sewing room, you need to shut it down. I am suggesting that, as you contemplate the future, you carefully evaluate the way you are allocating your time *now*. Choose wisely and your decision will reward you. Choose unwisely and your decision may rob you.

Your Assignment

Here is a short exercise designed to help you evaluate what you need to do with what you have just read. Get a notepad and write these four words in a list on the left side of a blank page:

Physically

Relationally

Professionally

Spiritually

Beside each word, write one thing you can begin doing that, if done consistently, would have a positive effect on that component of your life. What small investment in each of those areas can you begin making that you'll be able to look back on as a worthy investment of your time? What can you begin to do consistently—physically, relationally, professionally, and spiritually—that will have cumulative value? What do you wish you had done consistently over the past twelve months in each of those areas? Spending a few minutes answering these questions will provide you with a starting point for using your time more wisely beginning now.

If Job was right, and the number of our days really is determined, if there are limits we cannot exceed, then the issue of how we spend our time is of paramount importance. Indeed, time may be the most crucial arena in which to apply our big question. So once again let me ask: In light of your past experience, your current circumstances, and your future hopes and dreams, how should you be allocating your time? What do you need to add to your schedule? What should be subtracted? Where do you need to apply the principle of cumulative value?

Your time is your life. What is the wise thing to do?

Part 4

A Question
of Morality

Sex for Dummies

Why Aren't These People Smiling?

The simple message of these next few chapters is one I've spent thirty years of my life trying to instill in the minds and hearts of American teenagers. Some listened and applied. Through the years I have received countless letters and e-mails from students thanking me for this uncomplicated, yet profound principle. Many of these former students are married now and enjoying the rewards of having chosen the path of wisdom in this area of life.

Unfortunately, many more chose not to heed my warnings. And that's understandable. Every day, students are bombarded with messages and images that support a different viewpoint—a view fueled by the God-given passions raging inside their over-stimulated and underdisciplined bodies. Besides, I'm old enough to be their dad. What could *I* possibly know?

Nothing has stolen more dreams, dashed more hopes, broken up more families, and messed up more people psychologically than our propensity to disregard God's commands regarding sexual purity. Most of the major social ills in America are caused by, or fueled by, the misuse of our sexuality. If issues related to sexual impurity—adultery, the shrapnel associated with adultery, addiction to pornography, AIDS and other sexually transmitted diseases, abortion, the psychological effects associated with abortion, sexual abuse, incest, rape, and all sexual addictions—were to suddenly disappear from society, imagine the resources we would have available to apply to the handful of issues that would remain.

Since God grants us free will, there will always be people who will themselves into the complications associated with sexual impurity. This, too, is a fact of life. But for the sake of those who are willing to listen, the warning must be sounded.

Slow Learners

I started this book by saying that we have all done things we regret. We regret some decisions because they are embarrassing. Other regrets stem from decisions that ate up our time or wasted our resources. But no regret runs deeper than the regret associated with unwise moral decisions. In time you may find you are able to laugh about wasted money and poor time management. But when it comes to moral failure, time doesn't help. Nobody ever laughs about an affair, a divorce, a sexual addiction, or abuse. In the arena of moral failure, the regret runs deep and the pain can traverse generations. Chances are, your greatest regrets in life fall somewhere within this category.

The strange thing is, as predictable as the outcomes are, we don't appear to have learned very much. One would think that after losing thousands of people to sexually transmitted diseases and watching a generation or two of kids grow up without fathers in their homes, we might have learned something. But alas, lust and greed continue to drive us past the limits afforded by common sense.

I was reminded of how predictable certain outcomes are one afternoon while sitting in my chiropractor's waiting room. I struck up a conversation with a woman whose son was reading a book I had read, and she asked me if I was a teacher. When I informed her that I was a pastor, she launched into a detailed account of her unfaithful husband and subsequent divorce. When she mentioned that her husband had run off with his younger secretary, I responded, "Now that was original." Not dissuaded by my sarcasm, she went on to talk about how quickly he had married his mistress and how difficult it was to find a job that left her with the flexibility she needed to raise their middle-school-aged son.

I shook my head and said, "Well, let me assure you of one thing: Your husband is far more miserable than you will ever be."

She looked confused, as did the other people in the waiting

room who were pretending not to listen to what was quickly becoming a potential script idea for a new reality TV show.

"What do you mean by that?" she asked.

"Well, pretty soon your ex's new wife is going to want to start a family. He's not going to want to do that because he already did that once. She's going to be upset, and either way he goes, he's not going to get what he wants. One day he's going to wake up and realize that he is stuck."

Immediately, the guy to my left, whose nose had been buried in his newspaper, blurted out, "You got that right!" Apparently I had hit a nerve. But since I had already opened up one can of worms, I just ignored his comment and focused on my new friend.

She sat up a little straighter and actually smiled at the thought of her ex suffering for a change. "You know, I didn't think about that. But I bet you're right. And he's definitely not going to want to start another family."

Now she was starting to sound a little *too* giddy. Then she turned and said, "But how did you know all of that?"

"I'm a pastor," I said. "I've seen this played out more times than I can count. Solomon was right: There's nothing new under the sun."

She shook her head. "Yeah, I guess you are right. But when you're in the middle of it, you think you are the only one."

And there you have it.

When you're in the middle of it, you think you are the only one.

When the Fog Rolls In

Do you know why people are prone to make such foolish moral decisions? Because something always whispers to us that our situations are unique: *Nobody has ever felt this way before. No one has had to deal with what I have to deal with. I can handle it. I'm not like everybody else. The statistics don't apply to me. The statistics don't apply to my kids. I know what's best for me. My passion runs deep; love will keep us alive.*

As long as you're convinced that your situation and feelings are unique, you'll resist our big question. Now, that might seem to contradict the entire premise of the question—after all, your uniqueness is what makes this question so powerful. But in this context, we are not talking about your individuality as it relates to your past, your present, and your future dreams. In that way, you *are* unique.

But there is nothing unique about your circumstances, your emotions, your desires, and your passions. And as long as you deceive yourself into thinking that you are the first to feel what you are feeling, you will chase those feelings to the neglect of wisdom. And at the end of the day, you will discover that you are not so unique after all. The outcomes are predictable. Lonely is lonely, no matter how much money you make. Addicted is addicted, no matter who you know. Guilty is guilty, no matter what you drive. Depressed is depressed, no matter what you take.

It Cuts Both Ways

Now here's some good news. In fact, here's why our question is such a powerful ally in avoiding sexual sin, with all its complications and consequences: While the outcomes of sexual sin are predictable, the decisions that set us up to sin sexually are equally predictable. And—and this is a big *and*—our question will enable you to see those decisions for what they really are. If you're willing to face up to the fact that your temptation, circumstances, and feelings are not unique to you, this question will empower you to make choices that will set you up for success rather than failure in this crucial arena of life.

Again, the outcomes of certain behaviors are predictable, as are the steps leading to those behaviors. The sooner we face up to that humbling reality, the sooner we will quit trusting our hearts and choose to ask the indispensable question provided by our heavenly Father for those who want to look back with gratitude rather than regret.

Up until this point, you may feel like I've been circling the runway. So please put away your tray table and return your seat to its upright and locked position. And be forewarned, the next few minutes may be a little bumpy.

Hindsight

The Saga of Frank and Sheila

Think for a moment about your greatest moral regret. That night, that embrace, that purchase, that long glance, walking through that door...

I told you this might be a bit bumpy.

I know...it's probably something you work hard not to think about. You may have promised yourself you would never think about it again. And that may have been a good idea. But now that I've dredged it up, hold on to it for just a moment. There may even be a whole list for you to choose from. And they may not be in the distant past. Whatever the case, play along and pick one.

Now I want you to think back to the decisions preceding the event or relationship you regret most. At some point you have probably rehearsed some of these decisions in your mind.

I wish I had never taken that job.

I wish I had never called her.

I wish I had never accepted his invitation.

I wish I had never taken that trip.

I wish I had never subscribed to _____.

I wish I had listened to my mama.

If you think back far enough, you can probably string together a series of decisions that led you to the brink of the moment or season you now regret.

My point?

Our greatest moral regrets are always preceded by a series of *unwise* choices. Not wrong choices, not impermissible, not illegal, but unwise. We *choose* ourselves to the brink of disaster because none of the choices we make along the way are "wrong." So we don't hesitate. Then we defend our actions with the anemic excuse, "I couldn't help myself," followed by the equally ridiculous question, "How did I get into this mess?"

A more helpful and honest question to ask is, "How did I get *myself* into this mess?" The answer to that question is the same for everybody. *Everybody.* Once we follow our passions, there ain't nothing new under the sun.

How did we get ourselves into such messes? We made a series of unwise choices—unwise choices that sent us beyond the point of no return. The names and faces change, but the sequences and outcomes are tragically similar. We may think our situations are different and, therefore, what is wise for most isn't wise for us. But in the end…well, I think we've covered that sufficiently.

You know what's so ironic? When someone we know begins inching toward moral disaster, we can see it so clearly. Take Frank and Sheila, for example.

Office Party

Sheila and Frank work in the same office. Frank is married. Sheila's single. Sheila is attractive. Frank notices, but he's a committed husband and father—he made a vow and he plans to keep it.

One day while they're working together on a team project, Frank thinks, *Hey, I could ask Sheila to go to lunch. It's professional— we'll talk about work stuff.* He feels a slight twinge of hesitation, but he tells himself, *There's nothing wrong with eating lunch with a work associate. We've got to eat lunch. Besides, we'll be in a public restaurant.* So he shoots her an e-mail inviting her to lunch.

Sheila reads the e-mail and thinks it a bit odd that Frank would ask her to lunch. *He's married, for one thing,* she thinks. *I don't know what we will talk about for an hour. But what can it hurt? Besides, he is pretty influential around here, and there's certainly nothing wrong with having lunch with a coworker.*

So she accepts.

So far, nobody has done anything wrong or even out of the

ordinary. But let's be honest. How wise is it for a married man to go to lunch with a single female coworker whom he finds attractive? In light of his future hopes and dreams for himself and his family, is there any upside to this? And from Sheila's perspective, what can be gained from lunch with Frank? The risk far outweighs the rewards.

A few weeks later, the team is working late, and when dinnertime rolls around, Frank's thoughts turn to Sheila. She was easy to talk to and a lot more sophisticated than the guys in the group. Their profanity and stories of business-trip exploits always got on his nerves. He wouldn't have to endure all of that with Sheila. Again, there is a twinge of hesitation, but he sweeps it aside. *Everybody's got to eat dinner,* he thinks. *There is nothing wrong with having dinner with a friend.*

Sheila is flattered and hungry. Frank was easy to talk to, and since he is married, she knows she doesn't have to worry about him hitting on her like the less-than-subtle single guys in the group.

Do I even need to finish this? It is so typical. So predictable. And yet, up until this point, nobody has done anything wrong, illegal, or immoral. What Frank and Sheila (and their real-life counterparts) don't realize is that these are not individual, unrelated decisions they are making. They are on a path. They are moving in a direction—a direction that is obvious to everybody but them. And if you were to drop into their imaginary world and question them about their relationship, they would respond like all of us have responded at one time or another when confronted about the paths we trod: "I'm not doing anything wrong!" And that is deceptively true.

Later That Night...

During dinner, Sheila asks Frank about his family. *That ought to establish some safe boundaries,* she thinks. Unfortunately, things aren't going too well with Frank's marriage. When he tried to share his woes with his friend Denny the week before, Denny just shrugged his shoulders and changed the subject. But Sheila listens. She even asks questions. What's more, she offers Frank some good advice. *If only my wife thought more like this,* he muses.

Now what Frank and Sheila don't realize is that their relationship just moved to a new level. They have, unbeknownst to either of them, slipped across the border into the outskirts of intimacy. Have they been intimate? Nope. Nobody has touched anybody. If Frank's wife were to walk in, he could introduce her to Sheila with a clear conscience. But this conversation is the beginning of a different kind of relationship. And relationships almost always pick up where they left off.

As the team draws closer to their deadline, Frank's boss suggests that he split the team into three smaller groups so they can work on three components simultaneously. As Frank gazes at the list of people on the team, he has a decision to make. Should he pair himself up with Shelia?

If this were a movie, this would be the part where you would want to stand up in the theater and shout, "Don't do it! Run! Go home! Get another job! Think about your kids!" I wonder if God ever shouts those kinds of warnings at us? In the Old Testament, that was the role of the prophets. They usually ended up in jail, and the people they were shouting at usually ended up in trouble.

So here's Frank, staring at his list. In his mind, this is a small decision. Looking back, this would be the decision he would regret most. Looking in the rearview mirror, this would be the day he would wish he could relive. This would be the decision he would most like to take back.

He hesitates. Once again, something tells Frank not to do it. But hey, there's nothing *wrong* with working together on a project, right? The fact is, they have already been working together, and this isn't anything new. There is no logical reason *not* to. In fact, there are a half-dozen good reasons to do it. So he writes her name next to his.

Okay, let's get this over with.

One night Frank offers to drive Sheila home from work. She invites him in. When Frank crosses her threshold, their relationship moves deeper into the realm of intimacy. This time they feel it. There is nothing professional about any of this; this is all personal. But nothing happened. Nothing "wrong" or even "inappropriate." They chat for few minutes and Frank leaves. But at this point, you can stick a fork in it.

The next morning Darla asks Frank where he had been so late. And even though there was nothing *wrong* with stopping at Sheila's house, Frank doesn't feel it's necessary to mention it. Again, nobody has done anything wrong. Nothing has happened. But if Frank were to share it with Darla, you can bet your car *she* would think something was wrong.

Why? Because Darla is smart enough to know that relationships don't stand still. They are always going somewhere. She wouldn't respond to what had *happened*. She would react to where the whole thing was *headed*. That's how wise people (and suspicious spouses) think.

Two nights later the same situation occurs, but this time Frank embraces Sheila at the door. They both know it is wrong. But the wheels of rationalization have been churning for so long that their excuses overwhelm their collective consciences. And you know the rest of the story—a story with a disturbing moral.

Life Rules

Living Far from the Edge

The adventures of Frank and Sheila underscore an extraordinary, life-changing, future-altering principle:

Every poor moral decision is prefaced by a series of unwise choices.

The irresistible urge that neither Frank nor Sheila had the willpower to overcome that night on the front porch was the culmination of a series of unwise choices. The feelings they misinterpreted as love, fate, destiny, and all the other silly things that drive people would have been nonexistent if they had chosen the path of wisdom. Theirs was a series of unwise choices that set them up for the one decision that would send their lives tumbling in a new and unenviable direction.

Imagine if either or both had paused early on in their relationship to ask the $19.95 question: *What is the wise thing to do?*

What if Frank or Sheila had been willing to face up to what

was at stake rather than focus on where the line was between right and wrong? They had several opportunities to change the outcome of the story if either of them had been willing to ask and apply our question.

Again, every poor moral decision is prefaced by a series of unwise choices.

Got it?

Think once again about your greatest moral regret. Isn't it true that your decision to cross a certain moral line was predicated by a series of choices that led to that final and most regretful one? And isn't it true that you marched right along, justifying every choice with, *There's nothing wrong with…*

And you were right. There probably was nothing wrong with most of those preliminary choices. But looking back, it's all too clear, isn't it? One "nothing wrong with" choice led to another, until the temptation was irresistible.

Life on the Edge

So many things in our culture bait us to the edge of moral disaster. And because it is all legal, acceptable, and permissible, we take the bait. We read the magazines, pipe in the movies, stare at the pictures, laugh at the jokes, wear the clothes, and listen to the music.

Let's face it; purity is not a cultural value. Neither is modesty. While adultery is still frowned upon in most quarters, the impropriety that leads to adultery is actually encouraged, even celebrated. For the most part, teenage pregnancy is still considered a social evil. But again, the activities, fashion, and music that drive adolescents in that direction are not generally frowned upon. Parents fund the very activities that create the context for the act they consider so abhorrent. As long as we take our cues from the culture, purity and modesty will always be in the rearview mirror. Those lines will be crossed without a second thought. And once those lines are crossed, sexual misconduct is one easy decision away.

I was reminded of all this years ago when I was asked to participate in a task force designed to fight pornography. After about an hour of discussion, I raised my hand and asked what to me was an obvious question: "What exactly are we fighting? What *is* pornography?"

I won't pollute your mind or these pages with the definition I was given. Suffice it to say, the stuff I'm confronted with daily that I'm committed to not putting in my mind, the stuff I've tried to protect my kids from—these didn't even register with this group. What they were fighting was so far past the line of what I consider decent that I quit the task force. I remember thinking, *If that's the line of decency and acceptability, this war has already been lost.*

My point? Each of us, at a personal level, must scramble back to some long-abandoned standard of purity and modesty. If we don't, we will always find ourselves on the brink of moral disaster.

Culture has drawn the line of decency far too close to the edge. To accept the standard handed to us by our culture is to live and relate in a very dangerous place.

Our question, however, will lead you to a place of safety, a place where there is margin for error. Let me illustrate.

Politically Incorrect

I decided at the beginning of our marriage not to eat alone with or ride in a car alone with another woman other than members of my family. I made this decision based upon the experience of countless others who readily admitted that their extramarital relationships began with something as innocent as a meal or a business trip. I figured that by eliminating those two activities, I would be eliminating two possible contexts for temptation. Later I added a third component to my personal commandments: I decided not to counsel alone with women.

Whenever I share these decisions publicly, I watch men and women shake their heads in disbelief. For most people it sounds impractical, even insensitive. I would never suggest that everybody adopt my standards. And I would be quick to acknowledge that there is nothing "wrong" with any of the behaviors I have mentioned. But I would also be quick to point out that neither Sandra nor I have ever regretted my decision, even though it has caused some awkward situations with people who didn't understand and who took it personally. Through the years, I have met scores of people who wish they had adopted similar standards earlier in their careers.

Why go to such impractical lengths? Because every regretful moral decision is preceded by a series of unwise choices—unwise choices that don't raise an eyebrow or infringe upon our culturally programmed consciences. We all have certain lines we never intend to cross. But why draw those lines so close to the edge? Why set standards where the tug to ignore those standards is seemingly irresistible?

Men, let me ask you a really stupid question. What's more difficult, resisting the temptation to ask someone to lunch or resisting the temptation to embrace an attractive woman who has invited you into her home? Remember the "I couldn't help myself" excuse I derided in the previous chapter? Can you understand why this is such an anemic excuse for anything? Of course we can't "help ourselves" in certain situations. We have led ourselves to the brink of disaster.

Ladies, what is more difficult, saying no to an invitation to lunch or resisting the advances of a man you are infatuated with, a man whom you have invited into your home late at night after a couple of drinks? "But I would never let things go that far," you argue. Of course, you wouldn't. In fact, everybody who has ever allowed things to go that far never intended them to go that far. That's exactly why things went that far. Men and women didn't *intend* for them to, so consequently, they trusted their intentions to keep them out of trouble.

Wake up! You never *intended* to get yourself into *any* of the situations you now regret. Right? Your financial, moral, professional, and relational regrets all came about unintentionally. Nobody intends to blow up a marriage. Nobody intends to become buried in debt. Nobody intends to destroy a career. Nobody intends to be alienated from his or her children. Nobody intends to become addicted to anything. Your own experience substantiates the fact that intentions are pretty much a worthless defense against temptation and regret. It takes more than good intentions to cross the finish line in any area of life.

None of us plan—or intend—to get into trouble. The problem is, we don't plan *not* to. Adopting our question enables us to plan not to. It puts feet to our intentions. It gives us traction to stand our ground against the seemingly overwhelming current of culture.

Here's how it works.

Extreme Measures

Playing It Safe

Our question will lead you away from the brink of a decision you may regret to a place of safety. This fact alone is why it's so easy to disregard this question in the arena of sexuality. Like you, I don't want to miss out on anything life has to offer. So my natural inclination is to ask, "Where's the line between right and wrong?" Once that is established, I want to cozy up to the line and live right there. To do otherwise may mean missing out on something good.

At the same time, I don't want to do anything now that will haunt me in the future. And there's a part of me that wants to please my heavenly Father. So once I've recognized where the line is, I try not to cross it. The problem with this approach is that there is no margin for error. In most areas of life, that is not a problem. If the speed limit is fifty-five miles per hour, I drive fifty-five miles per hour. If my thoughts drift and I find myself roaring down the highway at sixty miles per hour, no harm done. I just ease off the gas. When I was sixteen and my curfew was midnight, I tried to time it so that I arrived home right at midnight. I gave myself no margin for error. If I was a few minutes late, no problem, no consequences. If you violate the guidelines of your diet for a day, no problem. You just ease back into your routine the following day.

But when you cross certain lines sexually, there are always consequences, sometimes for the rest of your life. Slipping over "the line" in this particular arena of life can mean kids growing up without a dad in the home. It can result in women fending for themselves financially while trying to raise their children. It means men living with the constant distraction of images they can't erase from their minds. It means young women losing the opportunity to give themselves wholly to their husbands on their wedding nights. It means men constantly struggling not to compare their wives to other women they have slept with in the past. It can mean living with the burden of an incurable disease. As in the case of three friends of mine, crossing certain lines sexually can mean death—death that leaves a hole in a family, a mother mourning the loss of a child, brothers and sisters devastated. In the case of the HIV epidemic in Africa, crossing certain lines morally has resulted in hundreds of thousands of homeless children.

Let me be blunt. To leave yourself no margin for error morally is about the most insensitive thing you can do to those you love.

Relationally, it is a death wish. It is the worst kind of arrogance. It is tantamount to a recovering alcoholic walking into a bar and sitting down on a barstool, all the while justifying his actions with the excuse, "There's nothing wrong with being here as long as I'm not drinking."

Stepping Back

Wisdom would dictate that we establish some artificial boundaries a safe distance away from the moral point of no return. Boundaries so far from the brink of disaster that, should you violate one, the consequences would be minimal. Thus, my decision not to be alone with women in certain environments.

I hesitate to include this next example lest you think I'm a total societal reject. But you're more than halfway through the book now, so you might as well finish. And let me qualify this by saying that I'm not suggesting anybody follow my lead on this. It's just an example of something I did based on what I thought was wise for me.

I didn't own a television until I was thirty.

Am I a freak or what?

I lived alone during graduate school, and I knew what a subscription to cable would pipe into my apartment. I didn't want to deal with the temptation, so I never purchased a TV. After graduate school, I bought a nice condo in Atlanta. My parents gave me a beautiful cherry-wood television cabinet. But I didn't purchase a television until four years later when I married Sandra.

I can't begin to tell you how many people kept trying to give me televisions. They would open up my cabinet and ask, "Where's the TV?"

"I don't have one."

"You don't *have* one?"

"No."

"We've got an extra one you can have."

No one understood and I wasn't about to explain. But I knew from experience that it was easier to resist the temptation to buy a television than it was to control what I watched. Do you think I now regret that decision? Do you suppose I look back on those ten years and think how much richer my life would have been if only I'd had a television all that time? Not for a second. Would it have been *wrong* for me to own a television? Nope. But knowing what I knew then, I felt it would be unwise. Knowing what I know now, I think it was one of the best decisions I ever made.

Extreme? Yes. But in light of the extreme consequences of a moral failure, isn't extreme precaution appropriate? Let's turn it around and look at it through a different set of lenses.

How extreme do you want your current or future spouse to be when it comes to protecting himself or herself from unnecessary temptation in this arena? You may want to close the book and think about that for a few minutes. Your answer to this question will help you cut through the fog of self-deception. After all, what's appropriate for your spouse is certainly appropriate for you.

Try this. To what extreme would you be willing to go to protect your children from having to navigate the complexities of a home divided over someone's sexual impropriety, be it adultery or a sexual addiction? What precautions would you be willing to take in order to ensure that they never have to suffer through the emotional complications of a broken home?

In light of what is at stake, what is the wise thing for you to do? In light of what you want for your marriage and your family, what is the wise thing to do? In light of the extreme consequences associated with moral failure, what extreme measures are you willing to take? To what extreme are you willing to go to protect what's most important to you?

But What About...

Yes, people will chuckle, and your close friends may not understand. Yes, it will complicate things at times, and it will not always be convenient. And yes, it will send an unspoken message to your family about how important they are to you. No, you will never regret it.

Having waded with broken people through just about every scenario imaginable, I thought it might be helpful, if not meddlesome, to share the top five environments in which the seeds for moral failure are sown in the life of a married person. And let me go ahead and state up front, there's nothing *wrong* with any of these things:

- Chatting online with members of the opposite sex
- Dinner after work with members of the opposite sex
- Working with a personal trainer of the opposite sex
- Counseling with members of the opposite sex
- Ladies' night out dancing while husbands stay home

I've seen so much heartbreak stemming from these five situations that it is easy for me to eliminate these as options for my life. Especially number five. I never get invited.

Wisdom dictates that each of us sets standards that will keep us out of harm's way. These should be boundaries that are so far from the line of regret that, were we to cross one, we would suffer little or no consequences. When these are in place, a fascinating dynamic occurs: your conscience actually latches on to the artificial standard you have set. When you violate one of your self-imposed rules, you feel guilty. And that low-risk guilt serves as a reminder that you are venturing into dangerous territory.

Conscience Point

Some time ago I traveled to Dallas with Sandra to speak at a leadership conference. I'd been asked to come a day early to visit several radio and TV stations and do interviews to promote the event.

I was informed that a driver would pick me up at the hotel at 8 a.m. and escort me back and forth between stations. I assumed the driver would be a man. Never assume anything. Sandra, meanwhile, decided to spend that day shopping with a friend.

That morning I stepped outside the hotel at the appointed time to meet my ride. Parked in front of the hotel was a nice white Lexus with a woman sitting alone in the driver's seat. I thought to myself, *There's a nice white Lexus with a woman sitting in the driver's seat. I wonder where my ride is.*

While I stood waiting, the woman finally stepped out of the car and said, "Are you Andy Stanley?"

I said yes.

"I'm your escort," she said.

Suddenly I felt very uncomfortable. Why? Was it because it is a sin for me to be alone in a car with a woman? Nope. That wasn't it at all. I was uncomfortable because my conscience had become attuned to the standard I had set for myself. And she could tell I was hesitating to get in the car.

I didn't want to make things awkward for her, so I got in the car and we drove to our first appointment. And it felt really weird. As soon as I got the chance, I called Sandra and told her what had transpired. I sounded so stressed on the phone that she laughed. To make matters worse, the woman kept introducing herself to people as my escort. I, on the other hand, felt the urge to tell everybody we met that I didn't usually ride around alone with women. The truth be known, nobody but me really cared about any of that; nobody gave it a second thought. But I felt uncomfortable the entire day. And I'm glad I did.

Wherever our question leads you to set boundaries for your behavior, your conscience will take up residency there as well.

Perhaps you've begun to wonder if I'm overreacting just a bit...that maybe I'm taking this whole thing a little too seriously. And perhaps you are right. Maybe I am overreacting. But having talked to so many people who have underreacted and paid dearly, I would rather err on the side of caution. And, for the record, as I read the Scriptures, it appears our heavenly Father would have us err on the side of caution as well.

Flee!

The Wisdom of Flight

In Paul's letter to Christians living in the city of Corinth, a city known for its tolerance of sexual impropriety, he penned these words:

> Regarding sexual immorality, pursue all manner of sensuality and impurity, yet remain faithful to God and your spouse. Husbands, gaze upon women in a lustful fashion until your heart is full, but do not touch that which is forbidden. Wives, dress in a manner that provokes the lustful passions of the men around you, but in your actions remain faithful to your husband.

That's from 3 Corinthians, the lost epistle.

Just kidding. Go ahead and look—it's not in there. But doesn't that pretty much describe our approach?

Actually, what Paul had to say was far more succinct: "Flee from sexual immorality" (1 Corinthians 6:18).

The Greek term translated *flee* means "flee." As in "run really fast in the opposite direction." No doubt you have fled from something in your lifetime—an oncoming car, your neighbor's dog, a linebacker, your big sister. We all know what it means to flee.

When I was in third grade, I shot my sister with a toy arrow. My dad took the arrow and began chasing me through the house. I fled. I ran into the bathroom and sat down on the toilet to keep him from spanking me with the arrow. Unfortunately, the lid was open and I fell in wearing my favorite footy pajamas. My dad laughed so hard that he couldn't spank me.

When I was in fifth grade, I was walking with a buddy across a pasture when we looked up and saw a herd of cattle stampeding in our direction. We fled. When we reached the barbed-wire fence, we dove underneath and rolled to safety.

There is a certain emotion associated with fleeing. Fear. We flee when we know we are in danger. Fear prompts us to flee. The reason we don't flee sexual immorality is that we don't fear it; we naively believe we can handle it. So instead of fleeing, we flirt with it. We snuggle up next to it. We dance around the edges. After all, we aren't doing anything *wrong*.

There's nothing wrong with standing out in the middle of an open pasture with a herd of stampeding cattle heading your way, either. No verse of Scripture prohibits such behavior. I have never heard a sermon on the subject. In fact, the United States Constitution protects your right to do so. But nonetheless, it is a stupid thing to do. And by the time you've learned your lesson, you won't have another opportunity to apply what you've learned.

In a Category All Its Own

Paul doesn't stop with his four-word warning. He goes on to make one of the most profound statements in the New Testament: "All other sins a person commits are outside the body, but whoever sins sexually, sins against their own body."

Sexual sin is in a category all its own. It is the most dangerous kind of sin. Anyone who has done any significant amount of counseling knows this to be the case. Sexual sin wreaks havoc with the soul, whether male or female. The shame runs deep and the regret runs wide, often seeping into every facet of a person's life. Long after men and women come to grips with God's forgiveness, those who have sinned sexually still wrestle to forgive *themselves*. I don't know why I bother to write this in the third person. We all know this to be true from personal experience, either our own or that of someone close to us.

So flee! Don't hesitate. Don't look back. Don't try to endure it. Don't flirt with it. Don't fool yourself. Don't try to be strong. Run! Like a coiled snake, sexual temptation has a considerable striking distance. You are never as safe as you think.

Fleeing 101

In light of your past experience, current circumstances, and future hopes and dreams, what is the wise thing for you to do in order to avoid regret in this area of life?

If your past is dotted with moral failure, then it would be wise to establish extraordinarily conservative boundaries. Your past points to the fact that you are more susceptible in this area than the average person; consequently, you can't be content with average boundaries.

Through the years, I have had numerous conversations with young men who have been very sexually active before coming to faith in Christ. From their past experience, dating was almost synonymous with sex—sex was pretty much the goal of a date. Coming to faith in Christ didn't automatically erase those leanings.

My advice to a young man or woman coming from that kind of past is always the same: Don't date for a year. I tell them to get out their calendars, look ahead one year, and circle the date. They always stare at me with the same look of disbelief. Some listen; some don't. Those who do come back and thank me. Those who don't, don't.

Why a year? Isn't that a bit extreme? Yep. But those who've taken the challenge will tell you that what God did in their hearts during that year prepared them to venture back into the world of romance with a completely different perspective on relationships. Many of these young men and women are happily married now. They consider their decisions not to date to be defining moments in their lives.

I know young women who went out and found female room-mates in order to have some built-in accountability. I know of young adults who moved back home in order to avoid unnecessary temptation. I know young men who have canceled their Internet services. These people, because of their pasts, took extreme measures in response to our question. And while their friends chuckled, they were set free.

You Must Decide

As we said earlier, this question enables us to plan *not* to get into trouble. Asking the question enables us to stand our ground against the seemingly overwhelming current of culture. Applied to the arena of sexual purity, it's a question that enables us to make a clean break with the past and move purposefully toward our hopes and dreams.

But to leverage this powerful principle, you will need to pre-decide some things. You need to predecide about what are and are not appropriate environments. If you are single, you need to predecide how physically involved you should become in a dating context. You need to predecide your entertainment options.

All of this might strike you as a bit overboard. Extreme. Maybe even legalistic. But here's what I know. When men and women and teenagers are confronted with the consequences of their moral impropriety, they all say the same thing: "I would give anything—*anything*—to be able to go back and undo what I've done."

Anything? Isn't that a bit extreme? They don't think so. Perhaps you, too, would be willing to go to extreme measures if it meant being able to undo certain moments of your life. So why not take extreme precautions up front instead of facing the reality that even extreme sacrifices on the back end won't erase the past?

If you don't decide some of these things ahead of time, somebody else will decide for you. If you don't have your own personal standards, others will force theirs on you. Everyone agrees that there are lines that shouldn't be crossed. You must conduct your relationships within the boundaries you have set for yourself in light of your past experience, your current circumstances, and your future hopes and dreams.

Had you adopted our question earlier in your life, perhaps your greatest regrets could have been avoided. If you adopt it now, future regrets can be avoided. It enables you to experience what God originally intended when he gave humankind the precious gift of sexuality.

A Designer Gift

In the beginning, God didn't just create the heavens and the earth. In the beginning, God created sex. It was his idea! Is God good, or what? Better yet, after creating it, he gave it to us as a gift! I know you've thanked God for a lot of things, but have you ever thanked him for the gift of sex?

He gave sex to us as a gift—a gift that comes with instructions. Contrary to popular opinion, the guidelines for using this Designer gift were created to enhance our experience, not diminish it. God is not against sex. He's all for it! The parameters he has set are evidence that he is for *you* as well. For within these boundaries a man and a woman are able to experience something that goes way beyond physical satisfaction. When sex is enjoyed the way God originally intended, the result is *intimacy*. When we ignore God's guidelines, we pay the price in the very realm sex was designed to enhance—intimacy.

So once again we find ourselves asking this confining yet liberating question: What is the wise thing to do?

In light of my past experience, what is the wise thing to do going forward? In light of what's going on in my life right now—the health of my marriage or the nature of my current dating relationships— what is the wise thing to do? And as I contemplate the future—the legacy I want to leave for my kids, the prospect of finishing strong in my marriage, the story I want to tell my future spouse—what is the wise thing to do?

No, it won't always be easy to do the wise thing. But you've already experienced enough of life to know that it will be worth it.

Part 5

Wisdom for the Asking

Hide and Seek

What to Do When You
Don't Know What to Do

Since I always read with a pen in my hand, I often write questions in the margins of a book. I am grateful when I later discover that the writer has anticipated my questions and addressed them. I imagine you have a question or two or ten that you hope will be answered before we reach the end of our time together.

One of those questions is probably, "What should I do when I don't *know* the wise thing to do?" Asking our question will usually reduce your options, but it won't necessarily single one out. So what then? What should you do if you are genuinely committed to doing the wise thing but you aren't sure which of your options qualifies as the wise choice?

Emotional Static

Wisdom is not always readily apparent. Often the wise choice is obscured by the emotion of the moment. Emotionally charged environments are not conducive to answering our question.

We have all made decisions in the heat of the moment only to regret them later. Excitement over a person, product, or opportunity will skew our perspectives. A good salesperson can engage you emotionally in a product. Emotions can make it hard to see straight, think straight, decide straight. This is usually the case when love, lust, money, or a crisis is involved—these are not emotionally neutral environments.

Most of the decisions we later regret are made when emotions are running high. My guess is that the decision you regret most was made in an emotionally charged moment: not only were you unable to identify the wise thing to do, you didn't really care.

But I love him!

Just look at her!

Three hundred horsepower!

Five bedrooms!

A 40 percent return!

No money down!

Negative emotions leave us emotionally out of balance as well. We've all made one or more unwise decisions in the throes of anger, greed, guilt, loneliness, or jealousy. The truth is, when painful emotions are running high, we don't really care about making wise decisions, and so we pretty much do what we feel like doing. We are drawn toward activities that distract us from our pain, and therein lies the problem. It is next to impossible to discern the voice of wisdom when our emotions are raging.

The Know-It-All

An emotionally charged atmosphere isn't the only influence that causes wisdom to elude us. Our ignorance—or shall we say, lack of expertise—can also put wisdom out of reach. There are decision-making environments where our lack of training or education or experience makes it next to impossible to identify valid options, much less sort through them. Unfortunately, our roles as parents, spouses, board members, business owners, etc., often leave us in the precarious position of having to make decisions in specific arenas that lie beyond our core competencies.

As a pastor I run into this all the time. I can't count the times I have sat in, and sometimes led, team meetings where I am expected to shape decisions regarding real estate, construction, sewer easements, rights-of-way, cash sweeps, collars, interest rates, and a plethora of other business-related issues. And each meeting ends somewhat the same way. After all the smart men and women in the room make their cases for whatever it is we are trying to decide, they all turn to me and say, "So, Andy, what do you think?"

What do *I* think? I think I need a vacation.

After twenty years of looking at financial reports, I'm still not sure whether parentheses on a P&L statement indicate good news or bad. My wife will tell you that I have a difficult time balancing my personal checkbook. And I quit helping our kids with their math homework once they reached the fourth grade. When it comes to numbers, I can pray for wisdom all day, but what I really need is an MBA!

Seminary didn't prepare me to make wise business decisions. Nevertheless, as senior pastor, I am responsible for the business of the church. It is my responsibility to make sure we are following the path of wisdom on the corporate side of things, whether or not it is something I am equipped to do.

Reaching Our Limits

Eventually we all bump up against our limitations. We find ourselves in situations where we are expected to make wise decisions but feel totally inadequate to do so. Parents, remember bringing your first child home from the hospital? Talk about inadequate. How about your first year of marriage? Remember the first time you closed on a house? You signed a hundred documents that you never took the time to read. Why? Because you knew you wouldn't understand them anyway!

So what should you do when you're supposed to know what

to do, but don't? What do you do when wisdom is just out of reach but everyone is looking to you, depending on you to know and do the wise thing?

I'll tell you what wise people do: nothing.

Wise people know when they *don't know* and are not so foolish as to pretend they *do* know. Eventually they make a decision and move ahead. But only after they have employed their best-kept secret.

Knowing What You Don't Know

The Best-Kept Secret

Get out your pen or marker because I'm about to let you in on the best-kept secret of wise men and women everywhere. This is how they became wise, and it is how they continue to appear wise. This is how they manage to make wise decisions concerning areas of specialty in which they have no expertise. This is how they manage to make wise decisions even in emotionally turbulent decision-making environments. Ready?

Wise people know when they *don't know,* and they're not afraid to go to those who *do know.* When wise people bump up against their limitations, they stop and ask for help.

This is the rule of thumb for wise men and women as it relates to their limitations experientially, academically, and emotionally. They don't deceive themselves; they don't pretend; and they don't act like they're smarter than they really are. They know their limits. They know what they don't know, and they make sure they know people who do.

This is somewhat counterintuitive. A wise man needing wisdom? That doesn't seem to make any sense. What's the use of being wise if you have to ask for advice? If you need outside input, isn't that evidence of the fact that you really aren't all that wise?

No. Wise men and women frequently seek the counsel of others because that's the wise thing to do. Solomon himself espoused this simple, yet often neglected, principle.

The Wise Guy

According to the Scriptures, Solomon was the wisest man who ever lived. As a young king, he found himself overwhelmed with the responsibilities that befell him. Then one night the Lord appeared to him in a dream and made him a rather unique offer: "Ask for whatever you want me to give you" (1 Kings 3:5).

Imagine that! God appearing to a teenager and offering to give him anything he wanted. What would *you* have asked for? Think about it: God offered Solomon a blank check and said, "Fill in the amount." Here's how Solomon responded:

Now, Lord my God, you have made your servant king
in place of my father David. But I am only a
little child and do not know how to carry out my
duties. Your servant is here among the people you
have chosen, a great people, too numerous to count
or number. So give your servant a discerning heart to
govern your people and to distinguish between right
and wrong. For who is able to govern this great people
of yours? (1 Kings 3:7–9)

I suppose I would have asked for the same thing. Well, maybe
not. In fact, "a discerning heart to govern" would have been about
the furthest thing from my mind. That probably explains why
God didn't make me the same offer when I was sixteen. But Solomon's response was exactly what God was hoping for:

The Lord was pleased that Solomon had asked for this.
So God said to him, "Since you have asked for this and
not for long life or wealth for yourself, nor have asked
for the death of your enemies but for discernment in
administering justice, I will do what you have asked. I
will give you a wise and discerning heart, so that there
will never have been anyone like you, nor will there ever
be." (1 Kings 3:10–12)

And so Solomon was given wisdom and discernment beyond that of any man or woman who had ever lived. He became the go-to guy for just about everything. He was an architect, poet, philosopher, scientist, scholar, theologian, and ruler—a truly amazing individual.

In the New Testament, you and I are encouraged to follow Solomon's example: "If any of you lacks wisdom, you should ask God, who gives generously to all without finding fault, and it will be given to you" (James 1:5).

This wonderful verse contains an important assumption and a powerful promise. The assumption is that there will be times when we don't know the wise thing to do; the promise is that God will provide us with the wisdom we need. But like Solomon, we must first recognize our need.

That leads us back to our question. The wisest man who ever lived insists throughout his writings that, instead of looking within our own hearts for the wisdom we need, we should pursue the counsel of others. In fact, Solomon had more to say about the importance of seeking wise counsel than all the other biblical writers combined.

Here is a random sampling:

Let the wise listen and add to their learning, and let the discerning get guidance. (Proverbs 1:5)

The way of fools seems right to them, but the wise listen to advice. (Proverbs 12:15)

Listen to advice and accept discipline, and at the end you will be counted among the wise. (Proverbs 19:20)

For lack of guidance a nation falls, but victory is won through many advisers. (Proverbs 11:14)

Plans fail for lack of counsel, but with many advisers they succeed. (Proverbs 15:22)

You have to stop and ask yourself why the wisest man in the world would put such a premium on seeking advice from others. The answer, of course, is that he was the wisest man in the world! *Wisdom seeks counsel.* The wise man knows his limitations; it is the fool who believes he has none.

My guess is that Solomon remembered how overwhelmed he felt the day he became king, how badly he needed wisdom beyond his years, how discernment seemed hopelessly out of reach. As wise as he became, Solomon never forgot that his wisdom had come from Someone else. And so even after God granted him extraordinary wisdom, Solomon continued to surround himself with trusted advisers.

Don't Leave Home Without It

No one rises above the need for wise counsel. No one. In fact, the more successful we become, the more we need it because there is usually more at stake in the decisions we make. Violating this simple principle sets otherwise successful people up for failure.

As I write this, a high-profile personality is battling to stay out of prison. The court case involves an individual accused of murder. This individual has admitted to making "poor choices" or unwise decisions. Even if a "not guilty" verdict is the outcome, the person's reputation will be tarnished for life. That tragedy—as well as this expensive, drawn-out court battle—could have been avoided if the individual had simply paused before acting. It's another demonstration of how our unwise decisions set us up for what follows. Nobody rises above the need for wise counsel, but many sure do resist seeking it out, which is ironic.

But this dynamic is not limited to those with celebrity status.

Everybody's Business

You Might as Well Ask

F ew people enjoy being told what to do. It's why we couldn't wait to leave home, to strike out on our own, to achieve independence. We resisted our parents' advice, and we've been resisting the advice of others ever since. To complicate things, we are especially resistant to advice in the three areas where we are most vulnerable—the three areas that typically prove to be the sources of our greatest regret: how we allocate our time, spend our money, and handle our relationships.

If you don't believe me, try giving your neighbor advice about how to raise his children. Or walk in uninvited to the office next to yours and explain to a peer how she could make better use of her time. If you're brave, try explaining to a guy who's buying a lottery ticket that he is throwing away his money.

Let's face it, most of us are hesitant to pursue counsel in the areas where we need it most, and we resist counsel when it is offered. And so in the three areas where we are most vulnerable, we are quick to lean on our own understanding and make decisions that are clouded by our own passions and ignorance.

Everybody's Going to Know

But here's an interesting slice of reality to consider: while you may escape having to listen to anyone's opinion about your decisions, you can in no way stop people from forming one. This is the irony of refusing to seek counsel. In many cases, once you have made your decision privately, the outcome will eventually be known publicly. At that point, people will inevitably form opinions about the wisdom of your choice.

We can convince ourselves that our private lives are nobody else's business. But the results of our personal decisions are rarely private. We often make intensely personal decisions about seemingly private matters, but the effects are felt in the real world and are generally visible to the public.

Everybody knows whom you chose to marry. Your friends know the size, location, and price range of your home. People know what kind of car you drive. Complete strangers know where you work and where you were previously employed. People know whether you went to church last Sunday. And it's no secret whom you choose to spend time with. And whether you like it or not, everybody you know has formed some kind of opinion about all those "private" decisions you have made. It's just human nature.

Before you get too indignant, be honest: you have an opinion about the decisions your friends and relatives have made as well. Don't you?

I can't believe she's dating that guy.

Why are they sending their kids to that school?

Don't they know about the zoning issues in this neighborhood?

He must have dressed in the dark.

There's one other thing to keep in mind about your so-called private decisions: not only are your decisions known and judged by others, but they also *affect* others. Every decision I make personally and professionally affects other people, every single one. They may seem to be private decisions, but each has public ramifications—repercussions that reach beyond my personal and professional life. As a pastor, every decision I make regarding our church affects a lot of people. The same is true in my roles as father and husband.

The same is true for you.

You are not the only person affected by your choices. Chances are, *your* professional and financial security are not the only things on the line when you make business- and money-related decisions, and we've already seen how the consequences of our moral choices can scar others. The news is filled with stories of how thousands of employees can be adversely affected by the foolish decisions of a few greedy executives. All of us know of families that have been splintered because of a decision made by a son or daughter—a decision made in the moment with no thought of how it might impact anyone else. We all know kids who are growing up without a father in the house because Dad made a relationship decision that he thought was nobody else's business.

It may have been none of your business whom your brother or sister chose to marry, but it has impacted your life in some way, hasn't it? As a teenager you convinced yourself that what you did with and to your body was nobody else's business. But you eventually discovered that the consequences of what you chose to do with your body impacted everyone who loved you.

Private decisions have public consequences.

So since your personal decisions will be seen by, judged by, and experienced by others, why not involve others to begin with? Why not benefit from the insight you will be judged by? While it is true that what you choose to do may not be anybody's business, it is equally true that much of what you do will *become* other people's business. They're going to know, they're going to judge, and they might even be significantly affected. So why not invite a few choice people into the decision-making process with you? It certainly won't hurt anything. In fact, it could make all the difference in the world.

Listening, Learning

The Lone Ranger Wasn't
Really Alone

Have you ever stopped and thought about the irony of professional athletes having coaches? Think about it. Why would a guy who can throw a ninety-five-mile-per-hour fastball over the corner of a rubber plate sixty feet and six inches away need advice on how to pitch from an older fellow who may have trouble *seeing* the plate from that far? Why? Because professional athletes know from experience something wise people seem to grasp intuitively.

Every professional athlete knows that he or she will never reach, nor maintain, peak performance apart from outside input. Granted, the superstar pitcher may be the one with the skill, youth, money, and fame. But none of that is enough to keep him performing at his peak. He needs a coach. He needs another set of eyes and another source of insight to help him judge his performance realistically.

Not coincidentally, men and women who consistently make the right moves relationally, professionally, and financially are those who seek input from others. Again, they know what they don't know and aren't afraid to go to those who do know. And this private habit results in very public success.

Incapable and Insufficient

You will never be all you're capable of being unless you tap the wisdom of the wise people around you. Sure, you may get by. You may even do better than most other people. But you will never reach *your full potential* without help and advice from the outside. This is true professionally, spiritually, financially, and even relationally. I say *even* relationally because it can feel so unnatural to seek relational advice, especially at the outset of a relationship.

Think about this. We trust our own feelings going into relationships, whether it's dating, marriage, or business partnerships. Then we cast our lots with lawyers and counselors when leaving those same relationships. Imagine how much pain and chaos would be avoided if people sought wise counsel during the early stages of key relationships instead of putting so much stock in their *feelings*.

Most of us know what it's like to seek counsel on the back end of a relationship that is spinning painfully out of control. Whether it is marriage counseling, pregnancy counseling, or family counseling, it is an attempt to address relational issues that at one time we thought were nobody's business. Again, we have to wonder how much of that could have been avoided if we had sought wise counsel *before* making the decisions that led to the need for wise counsel on the back end.

If you have kids who are old enough to date, you are probably all over this. There's so much you would like to tell them—so many warning signs you would like to point out along the way. You are convinced that if they would just listen to what you have to say, they could avoid a broken heart or worse. But alas, they're a lot like you, aren't they? Not really that interested in what somebody else has to say until things get so painful or complicated that they are forced to listen.

If asking yourself, "What's the wise thing for me to do?" is so helpful, almost equally as helpful is asking someone else, "What do *you* think is the wisest thing for me to do?" As a parent, there were times I would have paid big bucks to get my children to ask me that question and mean it. I'm sure my parents would have paid to get me to ask it as well.

Wise and Wiser

One of the realities of being a preacher's kid is that I grew up hearing stories about the complicated situations people had "behaved" themselves into. Looking back, I realize my dad had an agenda in telling me all those stories. I've done the same thing with my kids. If it has the same effect on them as it did on me, then so much the better.

The moral of nearly every one of these stories is, "They should have listened." People failed because they didn't listen to God, their parents, their friends, or some other voice of reason. Partly because of all those stories, I grew up with a healthy respect for sin. Actually, *fear* may be a better description. But I also grew up knowing that it would serve me well to *listen*.

Why not pause long enough to listen to the people who have faced what we're facing, people who have already been through what we're about to go through and are wiser for their experience? Experience *is* a good teacher, especially if it is other people's experience. There's no point in learning something the hard way if someone else has already paid that price.

I am a better husband because of the wise counsel I received before I said, "I do." Sandra and I have been much wiser parents because of the incredible insights we learned from the men and women we sought counsel from through the years. I know I am a much better leader because of the advice I have received from the seasoned leaders around me. I don't know if it is fear, insecurity, or wisdom, but I just don't make big decisions without outside input. I don't want to find out what I "should have done" after it is too late to do anything about it.

When we receive wise counsel *after* a decision has been made, it is nothing more than a reminder of how wise we could have been had we asked. But let's face it; sometimes we don't want to ask, do we?

For Him Who Has Ears

Some time ago I was wrestling with what I considered a complicated staffing decision. For several nights I talked Sandra's ear off about how complex this situation was and how difficult it was to decide what to do. I reviewed the pros and cons of every option. I expounded on my history with all the personalities involved. I vented my thoughts, my disappointments, and my grievances. But I couldn't decide what would be the wise move.

Sandra listened patiently. But it didn't take long for her to see what was really going on: I knew what I had to do; I just didn't want to do it. So instead, I just kept talking about it. And talking about it. And talking about it. Now, Sandra could have called my bluff, but she is a wise woman who knew it was more important to help her self-deceived husband make the right decision than it was for her to make a point. So instead she asked me, "Why don't you call Steve and see what *he* thinks you should do?"

Steve is one of the wisest men I know, especially when it comes to sorting out personnel issues. Furthermore, I had spent a lot of time with Steve. He had walked me through some truly difficult relational issues. In the process he taught me some invaluable principles that later became reference points for all my relational decisions. I had spent so much time with Steve that often I knew what Steve was going to suggest before he had a chance to suggest it.

Sandra knew that.

When she suggested I call Steve, I blurted out, without thinking, "I *know* what Steve would tell me to do." Sandra just smiled. Mission accomplished.

Face it. One of the primary reasons we don't seek counsel from the wise people around us is that we already know what we are going to hear—and we just don't want to hear it. After all, deceiving ourselves requires a lot of maneuvering, a lot of intentionally dodging the warning signs along the way. The last thing we want is the opinion of an astute individual who will see through our elaborate charades and call us on it!

Several years ago, a couple in our church asked me if I would perform the marriage ceremony for their daughter. I don't do many weddings, but I had known this family for quite a while, so I agreed. My last words to them were, "Have Debbi call my assistant, and we can set up some premarital counseling."

A few weeks later, the mother of the bride made an appointment to see me. That was a bit unusual, but I agreed to meet with her. "We love Debbi's fiancé," she told me. "We think he's perfect for her. But he's been married before, and I want to know what you think about that."

I asked how long ago the man had been divorced. She said he had been separated from his wife for two years. Once again I asked, "How long has he been divorced?"

"Three months," she said.

Then I asked a question I knew she didn't want me to ask. "How long has Debbi been seeing Tony?" She hemmed and hawed and finally admitted that they had met a little over a year ago.

As the conversation progressed, I realized why she had come. The mother of the bride was interviewing me. Before she subjected her daughter and future son-in-law to my premarital counseling, she wanted to make sure that I wasn't going to say or do anything to throw a kink in their plans.

I informed her that our church had a policy not to remarry anyone until he or she had been divorced at least two years, and that depending upon the circumstances, we might suggest an individual wait even longer.

She shook her head and said, "That's what I had heard."

A few weeks later, she called to inform me that they were making other arrangements. I wasn't surprised. But I was mystified. Why would a mother want to shield her daughter and future son-in-law from questions designed to help them think clearly about one of the most important decisions they would ever make? Who would be so foolish as to prioritize a wedding over a marriage? And besides, if Mom was so sure they were perfect for each other, what possible harm could come from their meeting with me? Wouldn't love find a way? Maybe not. Or maybe she wasn't as sure as she pretended to be. Perhaps there was something she didn't want to face. Perhaps there were some realities she and her daughter were working hard to dodge. And dodge them they did. They must be proud.

Mirror Check

As we saw earlier, the Bible has a term for the person who refuses wise counsel: *fool*. Solomon indicated how failure to listen to advice is "the way of fools" (Proverbs 12:15). In our culture it sounds harsh to refer to someone as a fool, so we soften it by saying, "He acted foolishly" or "How could I have been so foolish?" But the reality is, when we refuse to listen, when we dodge the truth, when we insist on having our own way—we're fools.

Wise people know when they don't know. The fool is the person who convinces himself that he knows more than he really knows and doesn't need to ask anybody anything. At the end of the day, the wise man breathes a sigh of relief; the fool, a sigh of regret.

Bottom line; when we resist presenting our options to the wise people around us for fear of hearing what we don't want to hear, we are fools. When we insist on ignoring the warning signs and pressing on anyway, we are fools. And in the end, we pay. Fools always pay.

SOS

God knows there will be times when you lack wisdom, times when you'll ask our question and come up short.

If you are in the midst of an emotionally challenging situation and circumstances require you to make a decision, go for help. Don't trust your judgment alone. Just as there are times when physical pain makes us incapable of caring for ourselves, so emotional pain can drive us to the place where we need assistance.

If you are being called upon to make a decision that is out of your league in terms of experience or education, get some help. Don't pretend. Don't fake it. Asking for help is not a reflection of your lack of wisdom. Asking for input is *evidence of* wisdom. When our question doesn't yield the clarity you need, ask somebody you trust, "In light of my past experience, current circumstances, and future hopes and dreams, what do *you* believe is the wise thing for me to do?"

After all, wise people know when they don't know and aren't afraid to go to those who do.

Part 6

The Best Decision Ever

Perfecting Your Follow-Through

Painting Inside the Lines

I n light of your past experience, current circumstances, and future hopes and dreams, what is the wise thing for you to do? What do the wise people around you consider the wisest course of action for you to take? These are two extraordinarily powerful questions that you should bring to bear on every area of your life. Acting on the answers to these questions will set you up to live a life with few regrets.

But therein lies the problem: *You have to act.* You have to follow through. For your heavenly Father to leverage our question in your life, you have to act on what you discover. In these final pages, I want to help position you for follow-through.

The Gallery

Many years ago, toward the end of a long day alone with the kids, Sandra marched everybody to the basement and announced that they were to spend the afternoon painting. She covered a big table with butcher paper, pulled out three small canvases, laid out assorted paints and brushes, and told them that *she* would let *them* know when they were finished!

"Paint what?" asked Andrew, who was nine at the time.

"Anything you please."

"I don't know what to paint," said Allie, who was seven.

"I don't even know *how* to paint," complained Garrett, who was eight.

Without giving further instructions, Sandra headed back upstairs for a well-deserved nap. Thirty minutes later she was awakened by a sound that she rarely heard: silence. No voices. No make-believe explosions. No crying. Nothing. The house was quiet.

Concerned, she headed down the hall to the basement door. No sooner had she opened the door when she heard, "Don't come down yet. We aren't finished." In mama-speak that meant, "Go have a few moments for yourself," an offer Sandra gladly accepted. Twenty short minutes later, she heard the pitter-patter of six precious feet scrambling up the basement stairs. "We're ready! We're ready! Come see our artwork!"

What kind of paintings do you suppose were waiting for Sandra at the bottom of the stairs? What kind of art would you expect from three untrained, unattended young children? Three masterpieces? Three introspective self-portraits worthy of hanging in a local gallery?

Why not?

Why is it you imagine unintelligible strokes of paint splattered all over the canvases, the table, and the basement floor? Why are your expectations so low when it comes to my children's artwork?

There's a whole list of reasons. What it all boils down to, however, is that untrained artists won't make the right decisions. Untrained artists don't know the principles and guidelines of painting. They don't know proper technique. Their motives may be pure and their intent noble, but if they don't know how to paint—well, you get the picture.

Playing by the Rules

There are rules and principles that govern every discipline. Music, architecture, law, education, medicine, athletics, economics, communication, construction, art, finances, accounting—in order to make wise decisions in any of these arenas, you need an understanding of the principles and laws that govern them.

Your accountant cannot give you wise counsel unless he or she knows the principles of accounting along with the tax codes established by the federal government. When you choose a doctor, you assume that person is an expert in his or her field of medicine—you assume this professional knows how the human body works and how to fix it when it quits working. If you hire a builder to build your home, you expect him to understand the applicable government codes and standards as well as the principles of construction.

For a number of years, I served as a coach or an assistant coach for my sons' baseball teams. I learned very quickly that knowing the rules and understanding the nuances of Little League baseball make all the difference in a coach's decision-making ability.

For example, in our league there was a five-run limit rule. That is, once a team scores five runs in an inning, their turn at bat is over and the other team automatically comes up to bat. In the sixth and final inning, there are no run limits; however, because of a time limit imposed on Little League games, very few of our games ever make it to the sixth inning.

In spite of the run-limit rule, the coaches in our league would typically arrange their batting orders the traditional way—all their best hitters batted first, and the worst hitters batted at the end of the lineup. But one day it occurred to me that under the circumstances they had it all wrong. If there is a five-run limit each inning, that changes the goal of the game. The goal should be to score five runs *every inning*. So I started arranging our batting order accordingly. Instead of putting our worst batters at the bottom of the order, I sprinkled them throughout the lineup.

Suddenly, we started scoring consistently every inning. And as a result of moving the weaker batters up in the order, something else happened in our favor: the weaker batters started hitting. Moving them up in the order did something for their confidence. We won more games that season than any team in the league.

You see, knowing the way things work makes you a better decision maker. Every decision may not be obvious, but knowing the rules and principles narrows our options and increases our chances of success. If you have ever worked with a professional decorator, you have seen this dynamic at work. There are dozens, maybe hundreds, of ways to beautifully decorate a room. But there are some combinations of fabric and furniture that just won't work, and a good decorator knows which combinations to avoid.

Years ago Sandra and I had a room in our house that we just could never make look right. One night when my mom was over, we brought her into our dysfunctional room and said, "Help! What do we need to do?" She moved two pieces of furniture, and it made all the difference in the world. Sandra and I stood there in amazement. We wondered why we hadn't thought of that.

Simple. My mom is a decorator. She knows the rules. She took one look at our room and diagnosed the problem. And that brings us to the flip side of this principle.

It Cuts Both Ways

Generally speaking, when we ignore the rules or principles in any particular field, we pay a price. All the day traders who were active during this or that economic bubble over the past decade will know what I'm talking about. No matter how many times we—um, I mean, *they*—were warned to take a long-term approach to securities investing, they just kept on churning their money for short-term gains. And when the bubble burst, a lot of people lost a lot of money. When you ignore the rules, you pay.

This is why people who represent themselves in court usually don't fare very well. They don't know the law. They don't understand courtroom etiquette. They have no experience picking or reading a jury. They don't know the first thing about cross-examining a witness.

I have a friend who decided to improve a piece of land by clearing some trees. He's not a developer. He's not a contractor. (But he has a great personality.) And consequently, he didn't know the proper procedure for improving property inside the city limits. He didn't know you had to have a land disturbance permit. He didn't know that he had specimen trees on his land. He didn't know he was supposed to ask the city arborists to come out and tag trees. He didn't even know there were such things as city arborists. But he does now.

He assumed he could do whatever he wanted to do on his own land. But he was wrong. He didn't know the rules. And after a dozen meetings with the city arborists and a couple of city council members, my friend ended up spending $40,000 to plant trees all over the city as a fine for violating several city ordinances. Next time he will know better. But that was an expensive lesson.

I bet you have a story or two yourself. I bet you wish I would get to my point. Hold on, we are almost there.

Hands On

Knowing the rules and principles of a particular discipline is not enough. To harness their power, you must submit to or apply them. When a surgeon performs an operation, he is submitting to the rules and applying the procedures of his particular specialty. No matter how skilled his hands, if he were to ignore proper surgical procedures, the results could be devastating.

Wide receivers can't cut out around the cheerleaders, come back onto the field, and catch a pass without being penalized. The best tennis pro can't serve the ball into the stands and expect to win. The Atlanta Braves can't put ten players on the field at a time. Professional athletes must submit to the rules in order to win.

In every field it is both the knowing and the doing that make for success. You must first know how things work and then submit yourself to those principles, laws, and techniques. It is what you know and what you do with what you know that make the difference.

So...

The Beginning
of Wisdom

An Act of Surrender

W hat's true in the realms of medicine, construction, accounting, and sports is true in the core dimensions of
your life as well. There are laws and principles that must be ad-
hered to if you are to succeed in the arenas of marriage, parenting,
personal finances, friendship, work, and time management. Some
of these principles are intuitive; others are not. But knowing and
submitting to these principles make all the difference in the world.
For it is within the context of these life rules that wisdom is found.
They inform the decision-making process.

Every time you give someone advice, you are drawing upon
your insight about how some aspect of the world works. Through

the years you have stumbled onto some of these laws and principles. Some you have learned the hard way. You may have been exposed to others through the wisdom of your parents and teachers. But you know a thing or two about how life works. There are certain bad decisions you can spot a mile away. You can see trouble coming. At times you have tried to warn some unsuspecting soul to get out of the way—just like somebody warned you in a previous chapter of your life.

With all of this experience as a backdrop, let me ask you a couple of questions. If I can't expect my children to create masterpieces on canvas when they do not know and submit to the rules and principles of oil painting, how can we expect to make masterpieces of our lives without knowing and submitting to the laws and principles of life? If I can't expect my mechanic to make wise decisions about the maintenance of my car without first knowing how the car works, how can I expect to make wise decisions about my family and finances without first knowing the laws and principles that govern these important arenas of life?

Let me take it one excruciating step further. How do you expect to make a masterpiece of your life if you are unwilling to surrender to the Author of life—the One who knows which textures and colors are best blended for the outcome you desire? How do you expect to make wise decisions regarding your family, marriage/love life, and career if you are not willing to submit to the promptings of the One who knows more about those things than you or I ever will?

In the Beginning

Perhaps it was this line of reasoning that led the wisest man in the world to pen these words: "The fear of the LORD is the beginning of wisdom" (Proverbs 9:10). Wisdom begins with a proper understanding of who God is and who we are not.

Don't rush past this too quickly. Throughout this book, I have challenged you to ask *yourself,* "What is the wise thing for me to do?" In the previous section, I encouraged you to broaden your audience to a few choice and respected friends. But to fully leverage our question, you need to address it to your heavenly Father. For he is the source of all wisdom, and wisdom begins by properly aligning ourselves with who God is.

Solomon used the phrase "the fear of the LORD." In this context, "fear" refers to recognition and reverence that lead to submission. You may want to write that down somewhere. Wisdom begins with the *recognition* of who God is. This does not mean simply recognizing his power and knowledge. This is recognizing that you are dealing with the one and only Creator of all things. God with a capital G. Wisdom begins when we rightly recognize God's position as God!

Proper recognition results in *reverence*. Reverence is the appropriate response to the One who created and controls all things. The practical side of reverence is submission. Those who recognize and revere the Father have little choice but to embrace his right to rule all that he has created. That moment of recognition and surrender is the beginning of true wisdom.

The Aha! Factor

Lest we lose sight of the highly relational side of our heavenly Father, Solomon restated his point in different terms. Here's how the entire verse reads:

> The fear of the LORD is the beginning of wisdom,
> and knowledge of the Holy One is understanding.
> (Proverbs 9:10)

Allow me to paraphrase this amazing verse for you this way:

> Wisdom begins when we recognize that God is God and
> then we respond accordingly. The proper response, of
> course, is surrender. Once we have surrendered, God is
> more than happy to reveal more and more of himself. And
> as we discover more and more of the character and nature
> of the Father, we gain greater understanding of the world

he has created. Our expanded understanding results in an improved ability to choose wisely. Thus, true wisdom begins with a proper recognition of who God is coupled with a proper response—surrender.

If the idea of surrendering to your heavenly Father scares you, consider this: you unknowingly surrender to his principles and laws every day. Every time you make a wise parenting decision, you are applying or surrendering to one of God's principles. Every time you make a wise financial decision, the same thing is true. Every time you submit your body to the knife of a competent surgeon, you surrender yourself to the laws of God. The surgeon is simply making decisions based upon his understanding of the way God created the human body. Every time you submit to a human authority, you are applying one of God's principles.

"But that's different," you argue. "I'm just using good judgment." That may be the way you see it. But if you are simply applying principles that existed before you chose to apply them, you are borrowing from—and recognizing the wisdom of—the Father. Think about it. We have discovered and leveraged principles of physics; we have explored and manipulated the genetic code; we have pinpointed and eradicated many diseases. Our forefathers harnessed high- and low-pressure systems and used them to travel across the seas.

Every single day we benefit from the way God designed things to work. Everything we claim to have created in our human endeavors finds its ultimate source in something God created that we simply discovered and manipulated. Every time we take a breath, we declare our dependency upon and submission to the Father physically. Why then would we hesitate to submit our wills? Why are we so afraid to surrender to him our relationships, our finances, and our careers?

A wise physician does not ignore the way God created the body. A wise accountant does not ignore the principles of mathematics. The beginning of wisdom is recognition of and submission to the One who designed things to work the way things work.

It's Mutual

One more thought on surrender: it is mutual. Mutual surrender, or submission if you prefer, is one of the most powerful relational dynamics. When two people pledge to put the other first, that is relationship at its best. This is true whether we're talking about a husband and wife, employee and employer, or parent and child. In a relationship of mutual submission, rank and birth order are irrelevant. The point is that each has pledged all that he or she is for the benefit of the other. In a relationship of mutual submission, there is nothing to fear—it is a relationship of trust.

Here's a bit of truth that ought to erase all your misgivings about surrendering to the Father: Before you were born, he submitted himself to you. On a wooden cross, God sacrificed his best on your behalf. He put you ahead of himself. Read these words with that thought in mind:

> You see, at just the right time, when we were still powerless, Christ died for the ungodly. Very rarely will anyone die for a righteous person, though for a good person someone might possibly dare to die. But God demonstrates his own love for us in this: While we were still sinners, Christ died for us. (Romans 5:6–8)

While you had nothing to offer, Christ died for you. He put your sin ahead of his own glory. In this way, he submitted to you. He met your greatest need at great personal expense. To do so, did he demonstrate his authority? No. His right to rule? Nope. Instead, he drew from his vast resources to demonstrate the only thing that would give us the courage to submit fearlessly, courageously: he demonstrated his love. And that demonstration stands as an open invitation for us to respond in kind. And so we are called into a relationship of mutual submission, knowing all the while that our Father took the risk and went first.

I know from my own experience that it is far easier to *believe in* than to *surrender to* God. It's easier to ask myself our big question than it is to sincerely ask it of the Father. But the Cross stands as a constant reminder that I have nothing to fear. God can be trusted. After all, he has already demonstrated his unconditional love for me.

The Best of the Best

In the end, here's what it all comes down to. Our willingness to ask and respond to this question depends upon our willingness to make an important decision—the decision to fully submit our lives to our heavenly Father. This is where wisdom begins.

What's true of my children in the realm of art is true of all of us in our lives, relationships, and finances. We know all too well what happens when we paint on our own, when we wave God off in order to choose our own colors, strokes, and textures. Each of us carries the scars, the memories, and the regrets of those seasons when our wills took precedence over his.

God desires that your life be a masterpiece that reflects his greatness and your uniqueness. But to create a masterpiece with our lives, we must submit ourselves to the hand of the Master. We must allow him to influence each stroke on the canvas of our lives.

So let me ask you. Have you made this decision? Have you fully surrendered all of you to all of him? Have you predecided to submit to his will before you know what he will ask? If not, I can't think of a more appropriate way to end our time together than to give you an opportunity to pray a prayer of surrender. There's nothing special about these words. It is the attitude of your heart that will make the difference.

> *Heavenly Father,*
> *Today I place myself under your authority. I surrender all of me to you. As you demonstrated your love for me through the death of your Son, so I desire to demonstrate my love for you through a renewed mind and surrendered will. Thy will be done in me. I surrender all. In the name of my Savior, I pray.*
> *Amen.*

Epilogue

t is possible to live life with few regrets. Regret-free living is found on the path of wisdom. So as we part ways, let me ask you one more time.

What is the wise thing for you to do?

In light of your past experience, your current circumstances, and your future hopes and dreams, what is the wise thing for you to do?

A wise man put it this way:

Those who trust in themselves are fools, but those who walk in wisdom are kept safe. (Proverbs 28:26)

My hope for you is that you would walk wisely and experience God's deliverance all the days of your life.

Study Guide

The questions in this Study Guide are for your reflection as you read through *Ask It*. Use them to help you get the most from this book and to apply it to your life.

If you're part of a group that's going through this book together and meeting regularly to discuss it, the arrangement here works well for covering the entire book in six weekly sessions. Notice that the questions below are grouped according to the six parts of the book.

These six parts also correspond to the six sessions of Andy's *Ask It* DVD series. If your group is planning to watch the video series together as well as read through the book, be sure to discuss each time how the video content enhances, deepens, and illustrates what you read in the chapters.

Part 1: The Question
(Week One)

Read the Introduction and chapters 1–7.
(These chapters correspond with the *Ask It* DVD series session 1.)

Introduction

1. Andy says that our greatest regrets in life could have been avoided if we had asked this valuable question and then acted on our conclusions. What particular appeal does this promise hold for you?

Chapter 1: Dumb and Dumber

2. What are some examples of particularly unwise decisions you've seen people make?

3. Andy states that while none of us actually plan to mess up our lives, few of us plan not to. What might be some examples of the kind of "planning" you believe could keep people from messing up their lives?

Chapter 2: A Most Uncomfortable Question

4. What are some common ways in which we tend to deceive ourselves into making unwise decisions? What causes us to do this?

Chapter 3: The Slippery Slope

5. Andy focuses here on Ephesians 5:15–17. What do you see as the most important and relevant teachings in this brief passage?

6. Based on what you see in Ephesians 5:15–17, how would you define wisdom as it relates practically to how we live our lives?

7. When we're contemplating a specific behavior or action, what's the danger of asking ourselves, "Is there anything wrong with it?"

Chapter 4: Climate Control

8. Andy asserts here that the culture around us is not "morally neutral" but rather morally and ethically perilous. Or, as Paul stated it, "The days are evil" (Ephesians 5:16). Are you convinced that this is indeed true about the times in which we live? If so, what convinces you of this?

9. Also in that Ephesians passage, Paul went on to tell us, "Therefore do not be foolish, but understand what the Lord's will is" (5:17). What do you think this understanding involves? How can we gain it?

Chapter 5: Stemming the Tide

10. Here Andy encourages us to add the phrase "in light of your past experience" to the question, "What's the wise thing for me to do?" What are some particularly important factors in your unique past that can help you make wise decisions for today and tomorrow?

11. How would past experience change the answer to "What's wise?" for various people? As an example, can you think of a particular decision or behavior that would be wise for one person but unwise for another— all because of his or her past experience?

Chapter 6: Seasonal Wisdom

12. Andy also encourages us to add the phrase "in light of my current circumstances" to the question, "What's the wise thing for me to do?" As you seek to make wise decisions, what aspects of your present circumstances are most important for you to be aware of?

13. As an example of this "seasonal wisdom," can you think of a decision or behavior that would have been wise for you at one time in your life, but unwise at another point?

Chapter 7: Looking Ahead

14. We're also to add the phrase "in light of my future hopes and dreams" to the question, "What's the wise thing for me to do?" As potential factors that should influence your wise decision making, what are your most important hopes and dreams?

15. What particular value do you think it might have for your life if you got into the habit of regularly asking, "What is the wise thing for me to do?"

16. In this chapter's closing pages, Andy asks, "As you evaluate where you are financially, relationally, morally, professionally, and spiritually, what would you do differently in each of these areas if you were to embrace our question?" How would you answer this question in each of those areas?

Part 2: The Alternatives
(Week Two)

Read chapters 8–9.

(These chapters correspond with the *Ask It* DVD series session 2.)

Chapter 8: Opting Out

1. As you face decisions in life, how easy is it to remember to ask, "What's the wise thing for me to do?" How fully

can you expect this to become a strong habit for the rest of your life?

2. In what kinds of situations do you most often sense a need for wisdom?

3. In the near future, what are some decisions you'll face—either large or small—for which you especially want to think clearly and wisely?

4. What are some examples you have observed of people who fit the portrait Solomon gave in Proverbs of a "simple" person?

5. What are some examples you have observed of people who fit the portrait Solomon gave of a "fool"?

6. What are some examples you have observed of people who fit the portrait Solomon gave of a "mocker" or "scoffer"?

7. For each of those three categories, what do you see as the strongest contrast with the wise person?

Chapter 9: Turn Around

8. What is your typical response to receiving correction from someone? How easily do you reach the point of being grateful for such correction?

9. Andy focuses on Proverbs 1:20–33, where wisdom is personified as a woman in the streets calling out to everyone. What stands out most to you in this portrait of wisdom at work?

10. As "Wisdom" speaks in Proverbs 1, she mentions the kinds of people who refuse to listen to her. What do you see as the most important reasons certain people reject wisdom, despite its proven benefits?

11. What evidence and examples have you seen of the lasting consequences for those who reject wisdom?

12. In your own life, what particular appeal do you find in the promise given in Wisdom's closing sentence in this passage (verse 33)?

Part 3: A Question of Time (Week Three)

Read chapters 10–11.

(These chapters correspond with the *Ask It* DVD series session 3.)

Chapter 10: Time Bandits

1. Andy states here that to simply recognize that our days are numbered (see Psalm 90:12) represents "a giant step toward becoming men and women of wisdom." Why do you think this is true? What practical difference could that make in how we use our time?

2. Andy also says, "Time is life." How fully do you agree with that assessment?

3. What is a good example of the cumulative value of investing small amounts of time in certain activities over a long period?

4. Another principle Andy gives is that neglect has a cumulative effect. What example can you give of how neglecting to give time to a certain matter brought about an increasingly negative result?

5. What are some examples of random things that we too easily allow to interfere with the truly important things?

6. Andy says that wasting time is the equivalent of wasting life. What kinds of things can cause us to lose sight of this truth?

Chapter 11: Live and Learn

7. Andy writes that we cannot make up for lost time in the truly critical arenas of life. How fully do you agree with that statement?

8. What example can you give of having tried to make up for lost time in some aspect of life?

9. Read what Paul said in Ephesians 5:15–16 about our use of time. How would you express this in your own words?

10. In the area of your health and physical well-being, what's one small investment you could make over time that, with consistency, would bring a positive result?

11. In your relationships, what's one small investment you could make over time that, with consistency, would bring a positive result?

12. Likewise, in your professional life—in your work and career—what's one small investment you could make over time that, with consistency, would bring a positive result?

13. Finally, in the spiritual area of your life, what's one small investment you could make over time that, with consistency, would bring a positive result?

Part 4: A Question of Morality (Week Four)

Read chapters 12–16.

(These chapters correspond with the *Ask It* DVD series session 4.)

Chapter 12: Sex for Dummies

1. Andy writes, "No regret runs deeper than the regret associated with unwise moral decisions." How have you seen this to be true, either in your own life or the lives of others?

2. Andy exposes our tendency in times of sexual temptation to think that our situations and feelings are unique. Why is this not true, and why is this attitude so dangerous?

Chapter 13: Hindsight

3. "Our greatest moral regrets," Andy writes, "are always preceded by a series of unwise choices." How

have you seen this to be true, either in your own life or the lives of others?

4. Consider the story of Frank and Sheila. At what points would you offer advice to either or both of them, and what would you say?

5. In exactly what ways were Frank and Sheila being unwise?

Chapter 14: Life Rules

6. What cultural pressures often keep us from acting wisely in the area of sexual morality?

7. What particular value do you see in having personal moral standards?

8. What do you consider to be the right criteria for evaluating a particular moral standard?

Chapter 15: Extreme Measures

9. There are always consequences, Andy explains, when we cross certain lines sexually. Why is this more profoundly true in the area of sexual morality than in other areas of life?

10. Andy asks a tough question in two ways: "To what extreme would you be willing to go to protect your children from having to navigate the complexities of a home divided over someone's sexual impropriety, be it adultery or a sexual addiction?" To put it another way, "What precautions would you be willing to take in order to ensure that they never have to suffer through the emotional complications of a broken home?" How would you answer those questions?

Chapter 16: Flee!

11. Look again at Paul's words in 1 Corinthians 6:18. What is the value and power of this counsel? Why is it wise teaching?

12. How would you explain the distinctiveness of sexual sin as Paul described it in 1 Corinthians 6:18?

13. How can we find and truly experience forgiveness for past sexual sins?

14. How does God ultimately want us to think of this gift of sex that he has granted men and women?

Part 5: Wisdom for the Asking (Week Five)

Read chapters 17–20.

(These chapters correspond with the *Ask It* DVD series session 5.)

Chapter 17: Hide and Seek

1. How exactly does an emotionally charged environment hinder the making of wise decisions?

2. This chapter speaks of the reality that we all reach the limits of our expertise in certain areas where we're expected to make wise decisions. What are some ways that you've experienced this?

Chapter 18: Knowing What You Don't Know

3. What are some ways in which you've especially benefitted from seeking the counsel of others?

4. Look again at 1 Kings 3:7–12, the passage Andy quotes that tells of interaction between God and Solomon, the new king of Israel. What does this passage reveal about both God's heart and Solomon's heart?

5. Also review James 1:5. What healthy attitude does this passage promote?

6. This chapter gives a selection of verses in Proverbs on the subject of seeking counsel from others. How would you summarize this collective teaching in your own words?

Chapter 19: Everybody's Business

7. What are some factors that cause us to resist the seeking and receiving of counsel from other people?

8. Andy mentions here that though we may make "personal" decisions in private, the results will generally become known publicly. Have you thought of this before? To what extent do you see this to be true?

9. Why is it important to realize how much our personal decisions affect other people?

Chapter 20: Listening, Learning

10. Andy states here, "You will never reach your full potential without help and advice from the outside." Do you agree? To what extent are you convinced that this is true in your own life? In what particular areas of your life is it most true?

Part 6: The Best Decision Ever (Week Six)

Read chapters 21–22 and the Epilogue.

(These chapters correspond with the *Ask It* DVD series session 6.)

Chapter 21: Perfecting Your Follow-Through

1. Andy emphasizes the fact that certain rules and principles, certain laws and techniques, are present in every aspect and arena of life—and we have to know them

and submit to them in order to operate successfully in those realms. What are some of these important rules and principles that apply in your particular line of work, in your chosen hobbies, or in other activities in which you're regularly involved?

Chapter 22: The Beginning of Wisdom

2. What would you say are some of the most important rules and principles we must know and submit to in each of the following areas: marriage, parenting, personal finances, friendship, work, time management?

3. Andy links the most important rules and principles that govern life to God, the Author of life. Why is this connection so important to recognize?

4. Look again at Proverbs 9:10, which talks about the "beginning of wisdom." How does this truth relate to your own life? How does it relate to everyone's life?

5. In what practical ways do you see that God is the source of all wisdom?

6. In the biblical phrase "the fear of the LORD," Andy defines fear as being "recognition and reverence that lead to submission." How would you describe fear in your own words as this term relates to you and God?

7. Andy speaks also of "surrender" as a proper response to God. What does such surrender involve? What is your reaction and response to this concept?

8. Andy also discusses the value of "mutual surrender" (or "mutual submission") in our human relationships. How does such an attitude reflect our trust in each other, as well as in God?

9. Andy points us in Romans 5:6–8 to the truth about the death of Jesus Christ and what it means for us. What application does this have for your life and your pursuit of wisdom?

10. Why is it harder to surrender to God than it is to believe in God?

Epilogue

11. Andy directs our attention to Proverbs 28:26. Why does living wisely require a certain lack of trust in ourselves?

Are you being sabotaged by your emotions?

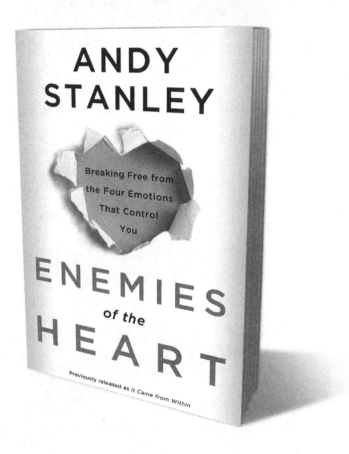

Andy Stanley offers fresh biblical direction to help you overcome the destructive emotions of guilt, anger, greed, and jealousy that can control your heart.

Good people go to heaven...don't they?

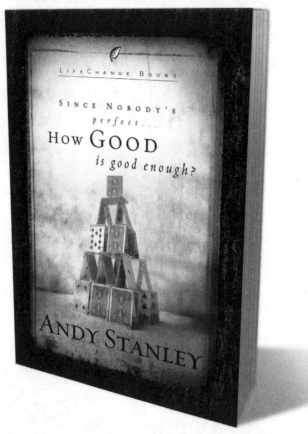

Surely there's more than one way to get to heaven? Best-selling author Andy Stanley addresses this popular belief held even among Christians. But believing that all good people go to heaven raises major problems, Stanley reveals. Is goodness not rewarded, then? Is Christianity not fair? Maybe not, he says. Readers will find out why Jesus taught that goodness is not even a requirement to enter heaven—and why Christianity is beyond fair. Andy Stanley leads believers and skeptics alike to a grateful awareness of God's enormous grace and mercy.